Religious Belief and
Emotional Transformation

Religious Belief and Emotional Transformation

A Light in the Heart

Paul Lauritzen

Lewisburg
Bucknell University Press
London and Toronto: Associated University Presses

BV
4597.3
.L38
1992

Associated University Presses
440 Forsgate Drive
Cranbury, NJ 08512

Associated University Presses
25 Sicilian Avenue
London WC1A 2QH, England

Associated University Presses
P.O. Box 39, Clarkson Pstl. Stn.
Mississauga, Ontario,
LSJ 3X9 Canada

The paper used in this publication meets the requirements
of the American National Standard for Permanence of Paper
for Printed Library Materials Z39.48-1984.

Lauritzen, Paul.
    Religious belief and emotional transformation : light in the heart
/ Paul Lauritzen
        p.   cm.
    Includes bibliographical references and index.
    ISBN 0–8387–5217–9 (alk. paper)
    1. Emotions—Religious aspects—Christianity.   2. Christian
ethics.   I. Title.
BV4597.3.L38   1992
241–dc20   91–55509
                                                                CIP

PRINTED IN THE UNITED STATES OF AMERICA

Contents

Preface

A candle of understanding shall be lit in your heart.
—II Esdras 14:25

The image of a candle of understanding illuminating one's heart beautiful-ly captures the central motif of this study. Traditionally the heart has been the organ that symbolized human emotion, while light has been that which reason produced. The metaphor of a light in one's heart, therefore, repre-sents a rejection of the putative dichotomy between reason and emotion; all the more so since it is a candle of understanding in one's heart, for a can-dle generates both light and heat. Reason (light) and emotion (heat) are here symbolically joined. The possibility of such a *rapprochement* between reason and emotion has framed this study. The question guiding the work has been this: What consequences follow for the study of religious ethics of rejecting the dichotomy between reason and emotion? From the start I have assumed that emotions play a more important role in the moral life than has usually been supposed, and that one cannot fully account for the impact of religious belief on the moral life without accounting for the rela-tion of religious belief and emotion. Both of these points, however, are obscured when reason is opposed to emotion. I have thus sought in this study to overcome this opposition; to show how religious belief is related to emotion; and to argue that attention to emotions is absolutely essential to philosophical and theological clarity about moral transformation. For this reason, it would be fitting to read this entire study as an extended effort to see how religion can light a candle of understanding in one's heart.

Few works that begin as dissertations ever fully escape the limitations imposed by this genre. This book is no exception. It began many years ago as a dissertation, and despite seemingly countless revisions and recast-ings, it still bears the stamp of its origin. It would be a better work if it were otherwise.

The fact that the book began as it did also means that I have more than the usual number of people to thank for their help and support. Indeed, I have been overwhelmed by the generosity of those who have given of their time and talent in responding to various versions of this work, among them: James Averill, Dan Brock, Paul Jerome Croce, Wendell Dietrich, Howard Eilberg-Schwartz, Donald Evans, Stanley Hauerwas, Jackie Lawson, David Little, Gilbert Meilaender, J. Giles Milhaven, Louis Newman, Susan Owen, John P. Reeder, Jr., David H. Smith, Sumner B. Twiss, and Lee Yearley.

I owe a special debt to Jock Reeder, who, from the start, was both an unflagging supporter and an honest critic. This book would not have been written without his help. Special thanks as well to Stan Hauerwas who offered needed encouragement at a crucial juncture, despite the fact that one thesis of this work is that Hauerwas's work is inadequate in at least one important respect. I hope that I will always be as generous as he was.

A number of friends have sustained me over the years, even some whose friendship was tested by being asked to read several versions of this work. Thanks to Lloyd Steffen, Tom Kelly, Kate Sonderegger, Amy Eilberg, and Rosanne Zeidenweber.

Two others have my warmest thanks. Louis Newman and Howard Eilberg-Schwartz have helped make academic life the joy that it is for me. Although I disagree with much that Richard Rorty has written, I have taken from Rorty the idea of intellectual inquiry as a sort of conversation. Thus I think of my writing as part of a conversation—and not the last word—with others who share an interest in learning, and I have been fortunate indeed to have such thoughtful conversation partners who are also close friends. They have helped me in ways too numerous to record.

A number of institutions have also provided support for this project. Both the Graduate School of Brown University and the Charlotte W. Newcombe Fellowship Foundation provided generous financial support during the period in which the original version of this manuscript was written. A summer research fellowship from John Carroll University and several teaching load reductions from that institution allowed me to work on revisions. Thanks especially to Dr. Sally Wertheim, dean of the Graduate School at John Carroll, for her constant support and to my chairman, Joseph F. Kelly, who has done whatever he could to free me to write. Thanks also to the helpful librarians of Grasselli library, especially Br. William Balconi, Caron Knapp, Nevin Mayer, Marcy Milota, and Mary K. Sweeny. John Carroll University has also generously provided funds for graduate assistants to help work on this project. Special thanks to Debra Marsey, who did a superb job of readying the manuscript for production.

Finally, I would like to thank my mother, Wilma Lauritzen, for everything she sacrificed to make this possible.

The book is dedicated to my spouse, Lisa de Filippis. In trying to find the words to express how much I owe to her, I have come to appreciate the power of this simple acknowledgment. To Lisa, *sine qua non.*

Acknowledgments

Quotations from *The Grapes of Wrath* by John Steinbeck, copyright 1939, renewed 1967 by John Steinbeck, are reprinted by permission of Viking Penguin, a division of Penguin Books U.S.A. Inc.

Quotations from *The Idea of a Social Science* by Peter Winch are used with permission of Humanities Press International Inc., Atlantic Highlands, N.J.

Quotations from *Human Agency and Language* by Charles Taylor appear by permission of Cambridge University Press.

Portions of this work have appeared in "Forgiveness: Moral Prerogative or Religious Duty?" *The Journal of Religious Ethics* 15 (Fall 1987): 141–54; "Emotions and Religious Ethics," *The Journal of Religious Ethics* 16 (Fall 1988): 307–24; and "Errors of an Ill-Reasoning Reason: The Disparagement of Emotions in the Moral Life," *Journal of Value Inquiry* 25 (1991): 5–21.

Religious Belief and Emotional Transformation

Introduction

Critics of contemporary moral philosophy might well argue that it is a revealing irony that one of the central debates in recent ethical theory was originally framed in a piece of obiter dictum. In a footnote to a discussion of the relation between virtue and obligation, H. A. Prichard noted that if we contrast the discussion of the moral life found in modern moral philosophy with, "any vivid account of human life and action such as we find in Shakespeare, nothing strikes us more than the comparative remoteness of the discussions of Moral Philosophy from the facts of actual life."[1] Prichard went on to speculate about the cause of this remoteness. "Is not this largely because," he writes, "while Moral Philosophy has, quite rightly, concentrated its attention on the fact of moral obligation, in the case of many of those whom we admire most... the sense of obligation... is not a dominating factor in their lives?"

This study grows, in part, from a twofold conviction: first, that Prichard was noting a fact of fundamental importance when he observed this disparity between actual lives and moral theory; and, second, that one of the most neglected aspects of the moral life as it is actually lived is the place of emotions in our lives. When emotions are ignored in discussions of moral theory, there cannot but be a jarring discrepancy between these discussions and everyday life. This work is premised on the belief that we must recover the theoretical significance of emotions in the moral life and that this task is especially important for religious ethicists who wish to understand how religious faith can transform moral experience. One of the fundamental convictions informing this work is that a careful examination of our emotions and of their relation to religious faith helps to account for the power of a religious vision of the world to bring about dramatic moral transformations. It is just such an examination that this essay seeks to provide.

This study, then, will examine the transforming power of religious faith as it relates to human emotions. The question this work will address can be framed succinctly: What is the nature of human emotion, and how are our emotions related to religious communities of belief and practice? Or alternatively, with a more specific focus: In what way or ways are emotions generated, shaped, and sustained by religious belief and practice? By answering these questions, I hope both to account for one of the most important ways religious faith affects moral experience and to shorten the distance between discussions of religious ethics and the facts of actual life.

When Prichard noted the distance between moral theory and actual lives and connected this fact to a preoccupation with obligation at the expense of attention to virtue, he was not suggesting that duty could be done away with in a study of morality. Rather, his point seems to have been that virtue and obligation are complementary aspects of the totality of moral experience.[2] Each encompasses a dimension of moral experience that is missed if one focuses exclusively on the other. Focusing on obligation and duty obscures the way in which the whole person is engaged in living morally. When Prichard talks about the vivid account of human life as is found in Shakespeare, he is pointing to Shakespeare's ability to depict the rich texture of a human life, the commitments, life plans, perspectives, dispositions, and emotions that define and give substance to a life. Focusing on obedience to moral rules or on the experience of moral obligation, he correctly notes, cannot do justice to how lives are actually lived.[3] Not only do some of those we admire most seem not to be preoccupied by their obligations, but some of the things we admire most about them seem unconnected to considerations of duty or obligation.

About this point, Prichard seems to have been right, and there has been growing concern during the past fifteen or so years among moral philosophers and others that Prichard's insight be accounted for in discussions of morality. Among at least two groups, one advocating an ethic of virtue and the other advocating a feminist ethic, there has been a call to move away from moral theories that focus primarily on duty. Both groups have claimed that an ethic of duty is inadequate to the complexities of the moral life. Although there are many differences between virtue theorists and feminist theorists, they share the conviction that moral theory has traditionally been too narrowly focused on obligations and duties and thus has not been able to do justice to the way in which the whole person is engaged in living morally. Significantly, both groups have also called attention to the importance of human emotions.[4]

Among the religious ethicists, many have wanted to claim that focusing on virtue rather than on duty provides a better framework for understanding the relationship between religion and morality precisely because doing so provides a fuller account of what constitutes moral experience. It is argued that when our focus is not on obligation and duty and when we are not preoccupied with moral rules and principles, we are free to focus on how religious faith can shape the whole person. It is not just moral rules and principles that are affected by religious faith, but a person's intentions, dispositions, attitudes, and emotions.

For example, James Gustafson, one of the most influential Christian ethicists of the last twenty years, has increasingly stressed the importance of accounting for the role of emotions in Christian ethics and of overcoming the dichotomy between reason and emotions if this is properly to be done. Indeed, it is possible to read the development of Gustafson's thought, from *Christ and the Moral Life* through *Can Ethics Be Christian?* to *Ethics from a Theocentric Perspective* as an extended intellectual journey toward the affective. In *Christ and the Moral Life*, for example, Gustafson introduces the notion of a Christian "perspective" and defines perspective, in part, as "values that determine . . . affective responses."[5] In *Can Ethics Be Christian?* he says that he is interested in how a person's attitudes, habits, and emotional responses so often appear to be of a "whole piece." This wholeness, he says, can only be accounted for by examining our affections and their intimate connection to cognition. "Beliefs, dispositions, affections, and intentions" Gustafson writes, "are clearly interrelated in persons."[6] This movement toward the affective is reflected in the fact that Gustafson now begins to talk about "sensibilities" or "senses" that are primarily affective but intimately connected with specific religious beliefs. "Each 'sense,'" he writes, "is correlated with certain dimensions of experiences of God and articulated beliefs about God."[7] Thus, for Gustafson, Christian faith can affect the sort of person one becomes by engendering and sustaining certain affective capacities corresponding to the articulated beliefs of Christian experience.

Finally, in *Ethics from a Theocentric Perspective* this theme is explicitly articulated. Indeed, much of volume one of this work is a more detailed explication of the claims made in *Can Ethics Be Christian?* that there is a "rough coherence" between religious beliefs and emotions and that it is this coherence that allows us to account for one of the most significant ways in which religious faith can affect the sort of person one becomes. Moreover, Gustafson now makes explicit the absolute necessity of overcoming the dichotomy between reason and emotion if this view is to be at all plausible. This is why Gustafson says that one of the basic convictions informing *Ethics from a Theocentric Perspective* is the view that, "in dealing with morality and religion as aspects of human experience it is best to consider seriously the interconnections between the affective, volitional and cognitive features of each,"[8] and that the distinctions often drawn between affections, intellect, will and appetite can and do "falsify the unity of the human self."[9] Indeed, it is partly for this reason that Gustafson says that he prefers the Reformed tradition in Christian thought for this theological tradition always emphasized the centrality of the affections in religious and moral life, and has "never set affections against cognitions." So Gustafson has clearly drawn attention both to the importance of accounting for emotions in the moral life of the believer and to the need for overcoming the reason/emotion dichotomy to do so.

Nor is he alone in this. Stanley Hauerwas, another dominating figure in recent discussions of Christian ethics, has also focused attention on the impact of religious faith on the whole person, including the impact of faith on one's emotions. Indeed, one reason for Hauerwas's prominence is surely that his work displays the way in which attention to virtue provides a context for understanding how religious faith may shape one's entire being.

Although Hauerwas has not fully developed the implications of this insight for an understanding of how faith may shape human emotions, he is clear that the categories of self understanding provided by Christian faith may have an impact on the affective life of the believer.

Since it is precisely this claim that we will explore in this study, I want to begin with an examination of Hauerwas's work. One of the problems with Hauerwas's work is that it does not treat in greater detail either the claim that emotions are central to the moral life or that a particular conception of emotions is requisite to philosophical and theological clarity about how the self is engaged in religious life. Nevertheless, Hauerwas's work does provide a context for understanding how religious faith may shape our emotions, and it also points to—even as it fails to develop—the importance of self-understanding to human affective life. Not only does his work provide a context for understanding how religious faith may shape our emotions, it also illuminates the importance of self-understanding to human affective life. Indeed, one of the most significant contributions of Hauerwas's work is that it calls our attention to the fact that if we are fully to understand the relation of religious faith to our emotions, we must attend to both the nature of the self and to the relation between emotions and self-understanding. In fact, I will suggest that one of the issues most fundamentally at stake in the debate between virtue theorists and duty theorists is how to conceptualize the self. I believe, for example, that the emphasis on virtue in recent discussions of religious ethics reflects, in part, a disenchantment with a peculiarly modern view of the self, one that highlights individualism and autonomy and that is typically associated with an ethic of duty.

On this reading, virtue theorists are committed to rejecting what Alasdair MacIntyre has called the "emotivist" self, a view of the self characterized most fundamentally by an emphasis on the autonomous individual who chooses an identity in isolation from the contingencies of historical existence. As MacIntyre sees it, an advocate of the emotivist view will typically embrace a conception of moral agency that emphasizes abstraction because such a view, on the one hand, understands the self as constituted through its choices and, on the other hand, is frequently combined with a theory of (moral) rationality that highlights universality. This combination leads to a view of moral agency that seeks detachment from the particularities of social existence. As MacIntyre has written:

> To be a moral agent is, on this view, precisely to be able to stand back from any and every situation in which one is involved, from any and every characteristic that one may possess, and to pass judgment on it from a purely universal and abstract point of view that is totally detached from all social particularity.[10]

By contrast, for those who have focused on virtue, the self is understood as primarily communal. On this view, the self is constituted in community and moral agency is characterized not by abstraction, but by particularity.

Although the debate between virtue theorists and duty theorists has not generally been framed in terms of a choice between competing views of the self, it seems to me that this disagreement about the nature of the self is at the heart of the debate. More importantly, this disagreement has consequences for how one understands human emotions. Where duty theorists have embraced an emotivist self, emotions have been relegated to the periphery of the moral life. Where the goal has been to achieve detachment and distance from the particularistic concerns of agents, emotions have been seen as obstacles to moral development. By contrast, where virtue theorists have highlighted particularity and community, emotions have emerged from the shadows and been given a more important place.

Ultimately, then, the contrast Prichard points to between an emphasis on obligation and an emphasis on virtue is important to this study because this contrast reveals another: that between conflicting views of the self. This latter contrast is important because how one views human emotions and how one views the self are intimately connected.

This connection between views of emotions and views of the self will need to be explored in some detail in what follows. We will see that Hauerwas argues that the self is constituted in community and that communities shape selves through the communication of significant narratives. Hauerwas's work does not, however, provide a philosophical theory of the self that would help us to understand how religious narratives may shape emotions. For this we will need to look elsewhere. I plan to turn to the work of the philosopher, Charles Taylor, for help in this regard. While Hauerwas's work begins to intimate the significance of nonemotivist views of the self to understanding the importance of human emotions, Taylor's work reveals this connection in full measure. Indeed, Taylor has convincingly demonstrated that the significance of the conflict between two competing views of the self is not limited simply to moral theory. According to Taylor, contemporary study of human behavior in general (in psychology, or philosophy or wherever) is decisively shaped by whether one approaches human nature according to a model taken from the natural sciences or with what Taylor calls a "hermeneutical" model.[11] According to Taylor, when someone adopts a natural scientific or "objectivist" model,[12] he or she will almost certainly view human agency as atomistic. On this approach, one should study human behavior as one studies, say, the stars: abstract from qualities characteristic of individuals in order to arrive at those qualities universally applicable. As Taylor puts it, on this view one posits an "ideal of the modern free subject capable of objectifying the world and reasoning about it in a detached, instrumental way" (HAL, 112–13). By contrast, a hermeneutical approach emphasizes how our very identities as selves are shaped, in part, by our own self-understandings, and how these self-understandings are historically particular and crucially constituted in community. Where a natural science approach emphasizes individualism and abstraction, a hermeneutical approach emphasizes particularity and community.

Whether we talk with MacIntyre about the differences between emotivist and nonemotivist views of the self or with Taylor about the differences between hermeneutical and objectivist views of the self, the key issue concerns the role of self-understanding in the moral life and its relation to human emotion. Any account of the self that does not provide a central place to self-understanding, we will see necessarily relegates emotions to the periphery of the moral life for emotions incorporate a sense of ourselves and our situation. Taylor's discussion of the contrast between a hermeneutical view of the self and an objectivist view thus serves as a nice complement to Hauerwas's work, because Taylor carefully examines both the presuppositions and the consequences that accompany these competing views of the self. We will need to explore, for example, why self-understanding is essential when attention is focused on human emotions; why, given an emotivist view of the self, emotions will be treated as peripheral; and why, given an adequate account of human emotions, self-understanding will not only be important for emotions, but emotions will be important for self-understanding.[13]

By drawing on Charles Taylor's discussion of human agency, I thus hope to shed light on the importance of correctly understanding the nature of the self, if proper due is to be given to human emotions. As we will see, Taylor demonstrates the importance of self-understanding to human agency as well as the intimate connection between self-understanding and human emotions. And both of these points are important if we are to recover the significance of emotions in our lives and to account for how religious faith may affect our emotions.

Taylor's work, however, is important for another reason. Not only does he demonstrate the importance of self-understanding to human agency, but, as I suggested above, he also demonstrates how important a hermeneutical view of the self is to the articulation of an adequate view of our emotions. This brings us to a second presupposition informing this work. I said before that one of the fundamental convictions underwriting this study is that an investigation of the nature of our emotions is central to the study of religious ethics, but there is another assumption at work here. This conviction is that the failure of writers in the West to properly understand the relationship between religious beliefs and emotional experience is not due simply to the neglect of emotions as objects of philosophical analysis, but also reflects the pervasiveness of the traditional Western view of emotions as fundamentally irrational, as beyond our control, as things with respect to which we are almost entirely passive.[14] This traditional dichotomy between reason and emotion has come under increasing attack over the last twenty years (in Anglo-American analytic philosophy) for its failure to do justice to the cognitive features of emotional experience, and the present work is premised, in part, on the belief that this reassessment of the dichotomy is important for the study of religious ethics. Indeed, it is important for anyone interested in what Clifford Geertz has called the synthesis of "ethos" and "world view" in a culture's sacred symbols. As Geertz has astutely noted, there exists a dialectical relationship between world view and emotions; not only do religious beliefs and practice provide order and definition to our emotions, but our affective life, thus structured by our picture of the way the world ultimately is (i.e., by our self-understanding), reinforces our world view by making it emotionally convincing.[15] It is an important part of my thesis that the failure fully to appreciate the cognitive/communal dimension of our emotional lives has severely restricted our understanding of this dialectic, and of its significance for everyday life. As a result, directing attention to the cognitive structure of emotions, to the way emotions are embedded in a community of discourse should help us to understand more fully the role religion can play in living morally.

For this reason, I will need not only to articulate a congenial view of the self, but also to sketch a more fully adequate account of the nature of emotional experience. Taylor's work provides us with a good start here, but we will need to go beyond Taylor's work. Thus, after examining Hauerwas and after exploring the importance of a hermeneutical view of the self, I will attempt to sketch an account of human emotions that is sometimes referred to as a "cognitive" or "constructivist" theory of emotion. On this view, emotions are understood to be, in part, cultural artifacts. That is, emotions are understood to be shaped by, and crucially dependent upon, cultural forms of discourse, such as symbols, beliefs, and judgments. On this view, emotions are not to be treated as biological givens, invariant from culture to culture, but as culturally mediated experiences dependent on self-understanding and thus shaped by the social matrixes within which self-understanding itself is formed.

With this as background, I turn to consider the emotions of anger and resentment. Assuming that emotions are largely shaped and defined by culturally specific beliefs and practices, I ask how we should understand emotions like anger and resentment. What would it mean to understand our anger at perceived injustice as culturally mediated and not as biologically given? I try to answer these and similar questions by inspecting recognizable examples of anger in our culture and comparing these to descriptions of "anger" taken from other cultures. Throughout this discussion I try to demonstrate the way in which anger and resentment in our culture are experienced against the backdrop of moral beliefs and practices that emphasize individual rights and claims to justice, and that these beliefs and practices are not everywhere the same.

Once we recognize that experience of "anger" is inextricably tied to particular cultural norms, to culturally particular beliefs and practices, we are in a position to see how the experience of anger may be transformed in relation to specific religious beliefs and practices. I thus conclude the study by focusing on how particular Christian beliefs about the circumstances of human life and history may affect the experiences of anger and resentment. By examining how religious faith may change an individual's understanding of himself and his world, and how this transformation in self-understanding may affect the individual's experience of anger, we draw near to the central goal of the study: to account for the way in which religious belief and practice may shape our emotions.

1

The Place of Emotions
in Religious Ethics

Since our ultimate goal in this study is to provide a detailed and plausible account of one of the ways in which Christian belief and practice can affect the moral life of the believer, we can usefully begin by examining the work of one contemporary Christian ethicist, Stanley Hauerwas, who has made strong claims about the transforming power of Christian faith. There is more than one reason for beginning here: not only does Hauerwas highlight the importance of accounting for how Christian faith affects the whole person, including our emotions, but he also underscores the importance of properly understanding the nature of human agency if we are to account for the transforming power of Christian faith. Beginning here, then, will allow us to see both that we must appreciate the significance of emotions in everyday life in order to understand how Christian faith affects the moral life of the believer, and that we cannot appreciate the significance of human emotions in everyday life without properly understanding the nature of the self.

Virtue Versus Duty in Recent Religious Ethics

As I indicated in the Introduction, the immediate backdrop to Hauerwas's work is a debate concerning the merits of focusing on the role of virtue in the moral life as opposed to focusing on moral rules and principles. Writing in the inaugural volume of *The Journal of Religious Ethics*, William Frankena attempted to frame the terms of the debate.[1] According to Frankena, the two groups can be distinguished primarily in relation, on the one hand, to the different terms in which each group makes moral assessments and, on the other hand, by the differences between the two groups in terms of the objects of assessment. The first group, those emphasizing the role of virtue, insist on the importance of what Frankena calls "aretaic" moral judgments, judgments more appropriately made of persons than of actions, judgments that include "aretaic" concepts such as "good," "bad," "virtuous," and "vicious." By contrast, those emphasizing the role of moral rules and principles have focused primarily on "deontic" moral judgments, judgments made primarily of actions rather than persons, judgments that include "deontic" concepts, such as "right," "wrong,"'"duty," and "obligation."

Although the differences between a virtue ethic and a duty ethic are often framed in this way, it seems clear that the differences between an "aretaic" and a "deontic" vocabulary and between assessment of action and assessment of persons are not so great as either to call for a decisive choice or to sustain a prolonged debate, not, at least, taken in themselves. As many have pointed out, however, Hauerwas among them, the differences here have been thought to be important because they have other consequences. Assigning priority to assessments of action, it is argued, has led to a preoccupation in contemporary moral thought with questions concerning the justification of action. And focusing on justification, it is further argued, has led to a false picture of the role religious belief has in shaping the moral life.

Hauerwas and Virtue Theory

Even a cursory review of Hauerwas's work reveals that this is the context in which his work should be placed. Hauerwas is passionately concerned that exclusive attention to epistemological questions has resulted in an overly narrow vision of the moral life. Yet, when our understanding of morality is thus restricted, when we are focused primarily on justificatory questions, we lose sight of the role religion can play in the moral life. In part, Hauerwas's point is methodological. If, when reflecting about morality, we are primarily concerned merely to provide justifications for particular actions, then questions about how religious faith may shape lives simply do not arise. As a consequence, Christian convictions will appear superfluous.[2]

By contrast, an ethic of virtue expands our conception of moral experience and thus allows for an integration between a person's beliefs about the world and his or her beliefs about the values and purposes that result in action in the world. This kind of integration is crucial for making sense of the notion of Christian ethics, and this integration can arise only when we "cease thinking of moral conduct primarily as an affair of obligation" and start thinking of it as an expression of the sorts of persons we are.[3]

Unfortunately, Hauerwas has sometimes spoken of the contrast between an ethic of duty and an ethic of virtue as if it involved competing and mutually exclusive moral theories. This is unfortunate because framing the contrast in this way diverts attention from the issue of genuine importance here, namely, that consideration of the virtues highlights the way in which the whole person is engaged in the attempt to live morally. Still, nothing in Hauerwas's work has to be understood as an endorsement of a radical distinction between an ethic of duty and an ethic of virtue nor do we need to worry about his arguments for so construing this distinction.[4] We can attend, rather, to Hauerwas's claim that we need to expand our conception of moral experience as a prerequisite for understanding the relation of Christian faith to that experience. Consider, for example, Hauerwas's strategy for overcoming a too narrow conception of morality. It is a two-part strategy, containing both negative and positive elements. Both aspects shed light on our effort to recover the significance of emotions and on the importance of our view of the self to this recovery.

Negatively, Hauerwas's plan consists of attacking any conception of morality that does not provide a place for a distinctively Christian ethic, and, as we have just seen, this means engaging primarily exponents of an ethic of duty. Because an ethic of duty focuses narrowly on rules and principles, and on the justification of these rules and principles, it fails, says Hauerwas, to account for how Christian faith engages the whole person in a distinctive way. His attack here is spearheaded by an assault on what he calls "the standard account of moral rationality." According to Hauerwas, since at least the time of Kant, ethical theory has been dominated by the quest for moral objectivity. Taking the scientific ideal of objectivity as their model, philosophers have tried to free moral judgment from the subjective beliefs, wants and desires of moral agents, and to ground them, instead, in some notion of "impersonal rationality." The result has been an emphasis on universal and impartial moral norms, from which moral rules and principles can supposedly be deduced. The hallmark of the standard account of moral rationality has been its appeal to the paradigm of scientific objectivity, and the result has been a preoccupation with two ideas: deduction as a form of moral reasoning and disinterestedness as the proper moral attitude.

Hauerwas's attack, then, comes in the form of a response to the three fronts on which he believes the standard account is the weakest. He argues that there are at least three essential ways in which the standard account distorts the nature of moral experience: (1) it places "unwarranted emphasis" on individual decisions in "quandary" situations; (2) it fails to account for the importance of "moral notions" other than rules and principles as determinative of moral experience; and (3) it relies on an "atomistic" view of the self that leads to the alienation of the moral agent from his or her interests and passions. Further, the distortions are related for the spell cast by the scientific model of objectivity inevitably leads to the attempt to reduce the central characteristics of the moral life to those of a system. Hence the proponents of the standard account attempt "to supply a theory of basic moral principles from which all other principles and actions can be justified or derived" (TT, 22–23). This in turn leads to a focus on moral decision making in an effort to identify the basic rules and principles. Finally, by concentrating on decision, the standard account fails to make sense of the formation of a moral self that continues through time because it is primarily concerned with how, in the resolution of moral quandaries, reason is to control desire when applying moral rules and principles.

Here we can see how a preoccupation with an ethic of duty and with the standard account of moral rationality that often accompanies this ethic obscures the complexity of moral experience that is evident, if one is not blinded by theory. What is fundamentally wrong with each of the three aspects of the standard account is that each truncates some aspect of moral experience. Focusing on quandary situations ignores the continuities of everyday moral life where goodness is displayed, not primarily through the decisions made in troubling circumstances, but in the recognition of particular circumstances as morally troubling. Similarly, focusing on moral rules and principles fails to do justice to the rich tapestry that is the moral life, a tapestry that includes, not just rules and principles, but stories, symbols, and metaphors among others. Finally, focusing on an atomistic self freed from the particularistic concerns of a personal and social history disregards the importance in the moral life of individual life histories and life plans.

Although the standard account is thus defective in a variety of ways, the quintessential flaw in the standard account is found in its view of the self. Because the standard account seeks moral objectivity, and because the paradigm for this objectivity is drawn from the sciences, the standard account has engaged in a strategy of abstraction in relation to the self. Trying to achieve the impartiality of, say, an astronomer, the moral philosopher working with the standard account has sought to abstract from the particular circumstances of individual moral agents, thereby insuring maximum impartiality. The standard account thus requires that we "view our own projects and life plans as if we were outside observers" (TT, 23). Yet, once such a process of abstraction is the norm, there can be no hope of any adequate account of the ways in which we acquire a determinate moral character and hence no possibility of accounting for how Christian faith shapes lives.[5]

According to Hauerwas, this tendency in contemporary moral theory to abstract from the particularities of concretely existing individuals results in a view of the self that is shadowy and insubstantial. It is to redress this inadequacy in the standard account that Hauerwas introduces the three major constructive themes in his work: narrative, vision, and character. Although I believe that each theme corrects one of the three distortions created by the standard account, what really unites the three themes is the role each plays in the articulation of an adequate view of the self, a view capable of accommodating claims about the transforming power of Christian faith. For Hauerwas, narrative, vision, and character form the three sides of a triangular wedge by which he introduces a view of the self that will make conceptual sense of the Christian language of conversion.

The Importance of Self-Understanding

Since the relationship of self-understanding to moral transformation is of fundamental importance to our study, it is worth looking briefly at these three constructive themes in Hauerwas's work. I said above that I believe that each of the three constructive themes redresses a particular deficiency in the standard account of moral rationality. To be specific, I think that it can plausibly be argued that an emphasis on the narrative quality of our lives provides an alternative to the preoccupation with quandary situations; that attention to the idea of moral vision offers a corrective to focusing exclusively on rules and principles; and that focus on character redresses the standard account's inadequate picture of the development and stability of a perduring moral self.

Since the theme of character is explicitly linked in Hauerwas's work to developing an adequate account of moral agency, let us turn first to this theme. The relationship between character and agency is clearly established in Hauerwas's book-length study of the concept of character. In *Character and the Christian Life*, Hauerwas tells us that what he is really interested in is "explicating and analyzing how the self acquires unity and duration" (CC, 2). Indeed, Thomas Ogletree seems to me correct when he suggests that what interests Hauerwas preeminently throughout his writings "is the sense in which character expresses a basic life orientation which gives unity and integrity to the self."[6] What is character? In *Character and the Christian Life*, Hauerwas says that character "is the qualification of man's self-agency through his beliefs, intentions, and actions, by which a man acquires a moral history befitting his nature as a self-determining being" (CC, 11). Or again in the same volume: character "is but the orientation we give our lives" and it "is the form of our agency acquired through our beliefs and actions" (CC, 21 and 203).

Whatever one may think about the adequacy of this conception of character, it is clear that Hauerwas is attempting to articulate a moral framework that can accommodate a more substantial view of the self and its development. For again, what Hauerwas is ultimately seeking is an understanding of the self that allows us an insight into how Christian convictions form lives.[7] The reason "character" accomplishes this task for

Hauerwas is that, on his view, character is but an aspect of the self. As he puts it in *Character and the Christian Life*: "Nothing about my being is more 'me' than my character. Character is the basic aspect of our existence. It is the mode of the formation of our 'I,' for it is character that provides the content of that 'I'" (CC, 203). To understand character and agency in this way, Hauerwas argues, does not "entail a denial of the ability to make objective moral judgments about others" (CC, 29)—to think that it does is to fall prey to the spell cast by the standard account of moral rationality—but rather it is to "attempt to broaden the phenomenology of moral experience" (VV, 69).

Thus, Hauerwas's attempt to articulate an alternative conception of the self in his discussion of character reveals how character truly is the conceptual center of his thought.[8] This theme unites both his negative comments about the standard account of moral rationality and his positive proposals concerning narrative and vision. Insofar as the standard account restricts rational reflection in morality to the assessment of judgments, and abstracts from the concrete situations of individual moral agents, a discussion of character inevitably reveals the inadequacies of the standard account. An examination of the concept of character also reveals the way narrative and vision are embodied in the moral life. The particular way in which an individual's "self-agency" is "qualified" is determined in large measure by the narrative and perspectives that serve to define the person's understanding of the world.

This exposition of Hauerwas's two stage attack on what he calls the standard account of moral rationality puts us in a position to see the significance of Hauerwas's work to the project before us. Recall that the whole strategy was designed to accomplish one goal, namely, to provide an account of morality that could do justice to the impact of religious belief on moral experience, and, in particular, to the ways in which Christian faith shapes a distinctive and coherent ethic. We can now see that, in relation to this objective, Hauerwas's use of the categories of narrative, vision and character serves a dual purpose. On the one hand, these categories remove some of the philosophical obstacles to the development of a distinctively Christian ethic by allowing for the expansion of the range of experiences relevant to morality; on the other hand, these categories provide the conceptual framework necessary to make sense of a common theme within Christian ethics itself: the power of Christian faith dramatically to transform the self. Moreover, what unites these two purposes is the conviction that I have suggested makes Hauerwas important to this study, namely, that we can only do justice to the impact of Christian faith on moral experience by showing how that faith affects the whole person, including one's emotions.

Duty and the Neglect of Human Emotion

At this point we can also see how it is that contemporary moral theory has been led to truncate moral experience by relegating emotions to the periphery of the moral life. There are at least two ways in which this truncating process is set in motion. The first is related to the standard account's obsession with objectivity and all this entails. Hauerwas draws out one of the consequences of this preoccupation with objectivity. He writes:

> At least partially under the inspiration of the scientific ideal of objectivity, contemporary ethical theory has tried to secure for moral judgments an objectivity that would free such judgments from the subjective beliefs, wants and stories of the agent who makes them. Just as science tries to insure objectivity by adhering to an explicitly disinterested method, so ethical theory tried to show that moral judgments, insofar as they can be considered true, must be the result of an impersonal rationality. (TT, 16)

Since this "impersonal" interpretation of moral rationality leaves behind the particular history of the individual, it also leaves behind those emotions that are crucially a part of that history (CC, 120).

In other words, one reason that the standard account cannot provide for human emotions is simply that emotions, like selves, cannot be understood in abstraction from particular social contexts. Moreover, because the tradition within which the moral theories dominated by the standard account developed generally embraced a dichotomy between reason and emotion, a dichotomy that understood reason and emotion to be mutually exclusive, there was additional incentive to dismiss emotions as morally irrelevant. This is so because the moral theories dominated by this scientific ideal have generally wanted to supply a foundation for morality capable of supporting universal moral principles analogous to the universal principles of physics. As Mary Midgley has astutely observed, the combination of these two factors makes it appear as if we must choose between reason and emotion. "The metaphor of *foundation*," she writes, "is disastrous; a building can only sit on one foundation, so it looks as if we have to make a drastic choice."[9] Unfortunately, because duty theorists, and almost everyone else who has embraced the standard account, have also embraced the dichotomy between reason and emotion, the choice has seemed clear: reason must be the foundation. Thus, duty theorists have attempted to ground morality on human reason, frequently leaving behind—and providing no significant place for—our emotions.

There is, however, a second reason why the standard account has tended to dismiss emotions as morally insignificant, and we can see this if we turn briefly to the work of the standard account's quintessential representative, Immanuel Kant. Although Hauerwas has pointed to the connection in Kant between the standard account and a scientific ideal of objectivity, he does not discuss the connection between the standard account and Kant's concern for what might be called moral self-sufficiency.[10] While it is true that Kant sought a sort of scientific objectivity for morality, it is also true that he sought to secure for the moral agent protection against any possible reversal of fortunes. In other words, Kant sought to make the moral agent invulnerable, because self-sufficient, by limiting the agent's reliance on others or on fate for his moral integrity.[11] This concern for self-sufficiency is clearly what lies behind the famous passage in the *Foundations* in which Kant writes:

> The good will is not good because of what it effects or accomplishes or because of its adequacy to achieve some proposed end; it is good only because of its willing, i.e., it is good of itself. . . . Even if it should happen that, by a particularly unfortunate fate or by the niggardly provision of a stepmotherly nature, this will should be wholly lacking in power to accomplish its purpose, and if even the greatest effort should not avail it to achieve anything of its end, and if there remained only the good will . . . it would sparkle like a jewel in its own right, as something that had its full worth in itself.[12]

The significance of Kant's concern for moral self-sufficiency to the disparagement of emotions in the moral life can be seen if we appreciate the way in which for Kant emotions stood as obstacles to the goal of self-sufficiency. For Kant, emotions posed a sort of double threat. Whether emotions are treated as external to the basic considerations of morality, and thus as largely amoral, or whether they are treated as internal to morality and thus as morally serious, they are problematic and threatening. Emotions are an external threat because on the traditional view they are fleeting and unprincipled experiences over which we have little control. As a consequence, emotions will be construed as obstacles to self-sufficiency for, on the one hand, they will often pull in an opposite direction from that which morality demands, and, on the other hand, they will be unreliable, even when they do push us toward moral fulfillment. In other words, because emotions have been understood to be either uncontrollable or unreliable, they have been shunned by those moral theorists who, following Kant, have sought self-sufficiency.

Kant clearly dismisses emotions for these reasons. Although Kant's view of emotions is considerably more nuanced than he is usually given credit for, he is, in fact, reluctant to assign emotions a place in the moral life because they cannot be fully controlled and they cannot always be counted on.[13] The importance of control is stated clearly by Kant in the Introduction to *The Metaphysical Principles of Virtue*. "Insofar as virtue is based on internal freedom," Kant writes:

> it contains a positive command for man, namely, that he should bring all his capacities and inclinations under his authority (that of reason). And this is a positive precept of control over himself; it is additional to the prohibition that man should not let himself be governed by his feelings and inclinations (the duty of apathy). For unless reason takes the reins of government in its own hands, feelings and inclinations play the master over man.[14]

Yet, even when emotions can be controlled, indeed, even when emotions work for the good, Kant is concerned that they are still too fleeting, too unreliable to be assigned moral status. He writes:

> Emotion always belongs to sensibility, no matter by what kind of object it may be excited. The true strength of virtue is the mind at rest, with a deliberate and firm resolution to bring its law into practice. That is the state of health in the moral life; emotion, on the contrary, even when it is aroused by representation of the good, is a momentarily glittering appearance which leaves one languid.[15]

We see here the dynamic by which emotions are relegated to the periphery of the moral life. Because emotions pose a potential threat to the realization of the moral agent's commitments and duties, they are treated as nothing but obstacles to be overcome in the pursuit of the good. Indeed, as the above passage makes clear, even morally benevolent emotions, such as compassion and sympathy, are suspect if one seeks complete self-sufficiency.[16] It may be the case that nature has been particularly niggardly in providing an individual with a sympathetic disposition or a generally sympathetic person may find his or her compassion absent at the crucial moment. In either case, one is not morally self-sufficient if moral fulfillment rests in any significant way on our emotions. A similar attempt to dismiss emotions as peripheral to moral deliberation and unimportant to assessments of moral worth also arises when emotions are construed as internal threats to moral self-sufficiency. That is, if emotions are treated as morally serious, if emotions are understood to be sources of genuine moral insight and reflective of genuine moral commitments, the possibility for conflicts of duty or conflicts of commitments is greatly expanded, and such conflicts are thought to be internally threatening. They are threatening because they place the moral agent at the mercy of luck. If irreconcilable conflict is genuinely possible, a situation may arise in which an individual is confronted with a tragic choice. She may choose to do x or she may choose to do y, but she cannot do both; and both x and y exert a claim on her. In such a situation, however one chooses, there may follow a sense of profound loss or regret, and this loss or regret may be either personal or moral.[17]

One may come to feel either that the goodness of the world has itself been diminished or that one's own moral goodness has suffered.

Thus, to allow emotions a prominent place in the moral life is to open the door to the possibility of tragic conflict much wider than if emotions are not so treated. Our emotional attachments are many and varied, and if even a small subset of these attachments is treated as morally legitimate, the number of moral claims increases dramatically, and with it the possibility of conflict.[18]

We see here a second reason why Kant would wish to disallow the claims of our emotions as morally irrelevant: To say anything else would be to introduce the possibility of tragic conflict. Indeed, we can now appreciate that, to this way of thinking, one of the most significant advantages of the Kantian insistence on impartiality in moral deliberation is precisely that an appeal to impartiality helps to factor out personal emotional attachments which could well give rise to potential conflict. If, when deliberating morally, we may treat as irrelevant our emotional attachments to friends and family, if we may discount our passionate commitments to our personal projects, then moral decision making will be considerably simpler than it would be otherwise, and the possibility of conflict will be greatly reduced.

Yet, whether emotions are dismissed out of concern for objectivity or out of concern for self-sufficiency, there is a large price to pay for their dismissal. A preoccupation with either objectivity or self-sufficiency frequently leads to a false view of human emotions and to a moral ideal of rational detachment that divides a person against him- or herself. Unfortunately, no theory of morality that requires such fragmentation can possibly do justice to the many ways in which religious belief affects the whole person, for, under such views, the moral agent is not whole. This is why an ethic of virtue is a necessary complement to an ethic of duty. Attention to virtue, with its accompanying emphasis on narrative, vision, and character does not demand such fragmentation. On the contrary, an ethic of virtue requires an integration of reason and emotion, for to be a person of virtue, to use Hauerwas's words, "involves acquiring the linguistic, *emotional*, and rational skills that give us strength to make our decision and our life our own" (CC, 115; my emphasis). Here, then, we see the importance of Hauerwas's appeal to the categories of narrative, vision, and character. The categories provide the framework for articulating how Christian beliefs and practices form lives, and this means accounting for how Christian faith affects the whole person, and for how Christian faith informs a whole life.

How, then, does Christian faith shape lives? Or more importantly for our study, how are emotions formed by Christian belief and practice? The answer lies in the way Christian narratives shape self-understanding and in the way self-understanding, in turn, gives form and substance to our emotions. The importance of narrative to self-understanding has been framed in a particularly striking way by Alasdair MacIntyre. MacIntyre writes:

> A central thesis then begins to emerge: man is in his actions and practice, as
> well as in his fictions, essentially a story-telling animal.
>   . . . [T]he key question for men is not about their own authorship; I can
> only answer the question "What am I to do?" if I can answer the prior question
> "Of what story or stories do I find myself a part?" We enter human society,
> that is, with one or more imputed characters—roles into which we have been
> drafted—and we have to learn what they are in order to be able to understand
> how others respond to us and how our responses to them are apt to be con-
> strued. It is through hearing stories about wicked stepmothers, lost children,
> good but misguided kings, wolves that suckle twin boys, youngest sons who
> receive no inheritance but must make their own way in the world and eldest
> sons who waste their inheritance on riotous living and go into exile to live with
> the swine, that children learn or mislearn both what a child and what a parent
> is, what the cast of characters may be in the drama into which they have been
> born and what the ways of the world are.[19]

To use Hauerwas's categories, we could say that characters are shaped by
narratives, and narratives shape characters because they provide categories
of self-understanding. This is important because, as MacIntyre points out,
before I can answer the question "What am I to do?" I must answer the
question "Of what story am I a part?" In other words, I must have some
understanding about the world and my place in the world before I can act,
and what provides that understanding is a narrative. Thus, when Hauerwas talks about Christian narratives training the self to regard itself under
the category of sin or about Christian stories enabling us to see ourselves
as sinful yet redeemed, he is pointing to the capacity of Christian faith to
form our self-understandings in fundamental ways.

In fact, we might summarize the significance of Hauerwas's position by
saying that his emphasis on narrative and character throws into sharp relief
the enormous importance of self-understanding to the moral life as well
as the necessity of properly construing the nature of the self if the importance of self-understanding is to be appreciated. Ultimately what unites
Hauerwas's negative attack on the standard account of moral rationality
and his constructive articulation of the themes of narrative, vision, and
character is his insight that one cannot do justice to the transforming power
of Christian faith without accounting for the importance of self-understanding and the nature of the self. What is most fundamentally wrong
with the standard account is that it adopts the "emotivist" view of the self
that we discussed briefly in the Introduction. Yet, this attempt to characterize the self in isolation from the particularities of historical existence is
precisely what we have seen cannot be done if we are to account for the
transforming power of faith. The self is what it is only through the par-

ticular stories that provide a sense of self-understanding. We need particular conceptualizations of ourselves and our world in order to sustain particular virtues, and this we cannot have if we take as our goal the elimination of social particularity.

In other words, we need a view of the self that is not emotivist and thus does not seek to eliminate social particularity. We need a view of the self that can accommodate the importance of narrative, a view that acknowledges that human action, and human life generally, cannot be understood apart from a narrative that gives the action or the life meaning and coherence. This is why the attempt to eliminate social particularity is so disastrous: it robs the self of meaning and coherence. "Particularity," MacIntyre writes:

> can never be simply left behind or obliterated. The notion of escaping from it into a realm of entirely universal maxims which belong to man as such, whether in its eighteenth century Kantian form or in the presentation of some modern analytical moral philosophies, is an illusion and an illusion with painful consequences.[20]

It is an illusion with painful consequences, because to strip the self of the particular conceptualizations of the world and itself provided by significant narratives is to condemn the self to incoherence.[21]

Although it may at first sound odd to say with Hauerwas that the self "is best understood exactly as a story" (TT, 78), an appreciation of the significance of narrative to self-understanding suggests that such a claim is appropriate, when properly understood. Moreover, to appreciate the significance of a self-understanding provided by the important narratives in one's life is to see why a strict ethic of duty, one that provides no place for the particularity of concretely existing individuals, must be rejected. We must reject such an ethic because the abstraction from social particularity demanded by such an ethic obscures the importance of emotions in the moral life. "The language of command," as Hauerwas points out, tends to be inherently occasionalistic with a correlative understanding of the self that is passive and atomistic" (CC, 3). Unfortunately, such a view of the self stands in the way of recovering a place for human emotions for emotions have their place in the intricate texture of a human life, a texture that is riven through the process of abstraction at the heart of an ethic of duty. When the goal of moral reflection is distance and detachment, the importance of emotions in the moral life fades from view. By contrast, when the goal of moral reflection is to understand how the stories which shape the self empower us morally, emotions have a decidedly prominent place. For this reason, our discussion of the place of narrative in the moral life is important to the present study. This discussion draws our attention to the intimate connection between self-understanding and human emotions and, by extension, to the way in which religious narratives may shape emotions. In this, Hauerwas's work has been helpful. Nevertheless, we need to fill out Hauerwas's work by examining at closer range the intimate relation between self-understanding and human emotion. It is to this task that I next turn.

2

Emotions, Self-Understanding, and Religious Ethics

I have just suggested that in order to fully appreciate the significance of the relation between religious life and emotional transformation, we need to examine in greater detail the notion of self-understanding and the relation of self-understanding to emotional experience. Ultimately, we seek a philosophical theory of the self that will help us to make sense of the claim that religious narratives may shape emotions by shaping self-understanding. We have just seen that any account of moral agency which requires us to abstract from the particularities of human social existence cannot do justice to the role played by religious narratives in the moral life; nor can it allow a significant place to human emotions. But what alternatives exist here? What account of human agency and of the self will be adequate to the task of displaying the relation between religious narrative and our emotions?

To answer these questions, I now turn to the work of Charles Taylor, a philosopher for whom the connection between self-understanding and human agency has been central. Taylor makes it clear that how one approaches self-understanding is decisive for any study of human behavior. The options here are largely determined by whether one chooses to make self-understanding of central importance or to make self-understanding marginal. Taylor argues powerfully that the latter option is disastrous and eliminates any hope of accurately characterizing the nature of human agency, including moral agency. Taylor's discussion thus provides an instructive complement to our previous discussion of the role of character and narrative in the religious transformation of the moral life.

Objectification and the Eclipse of Self-Understanding

The works of Taylor in which we are primarily interested are a series of essays written during approximately the last twenty-five years and recently collected as volumes one and two of his philosophical papers.[1] As Taylor indicates in the Introduction to these collections, his essays during this period are unified by a common agenda: they all seek to argue against "an influential family of theories" in the study of human behavior that takes as its model the natural sciences. Because he is opposing a family of theories, his studies have ranged widely. They have included essays in political theory, psychology, philosophy of mind, and philosophy of language, among others. Yet, despite the apparent diversity, there is indeed a unifying theme, and it is that to model the study of humans on the natural sciences is radically mistaken. The essays with which we are concerned seek to track the variety of ways in which the natural science model is distorting, why the model holds such evident attraction for us, and what alternative models are available.

Taylor's studies help us to see that the central distortion of applying the natural science model to the study of human behavior is the eclipse of the role played by self-understanding in human life. To appreciate why the natural science model results in this eclipse, we must keep in mind the fundamental nature of the scientific revolution of the seventeenth century. Preeminently, this revolution involved a rejection of a world view that understood the cosmos as a meaningful order and the replacement of this world view with a conception of the cosmos as objective process (HAL, 224). This objectification of the world, this rejection of the universe as a hierarchy of meaning, meant, of course, that one had to approach the study of nature according to a new plan. No longer could one seek meaning through a study of nature, for nature was now divested of meaning. On the contrary, on the new scientific model, an individual approached nature, not in a quest for meaning, but rather in search of facts that would ultimately facilitate manipulation and control of the world (HAL, 134). Because the study of nature was now seen as the study of a neutral domain of facts, the appropriate methodological stance was that of neutrality and objectivity. Understanding the world of nature thus involved ridding nature of anthropocentric properties, and, in turn, this involved objectivity, detachment, and neutrality on the part of the investigator.

In identifying the problems that this turn to neutrality created, it is important to acknowledge the power of this view of nature and the staggering scientific and technological accomplishments that are the fruits of this view. Still, there are problems that emerge when this model of understanding nature is carried over to our attempts to understand human behavior. What all such attempts have in common is that they are inherently reductive.

And what they seek to eliminate is the role self-understanding plays in human life. We can see why this is so. Following the lead of the natural scientists, many social scientists have wanted to claim that just as the world of nature can be approached as a domain of neutral facts, so, too, can the world of human action. On this view, it follows that just as the natural scientist attempts to understand the world of nature apart from anthropocentric or subjective properties, so, too, should the social scientist attempt to understand human nature apart from subjective properties. Yet, to understand human life apart from subjective properties is just to understand it apart from self-understanding. Thus does self-understanding get eclipsed as the whole world, human actions included, is objectified.

Emotivist Versus Hermeneutical Views of the Self

One consequence of this attempt to objectify human behavior is the development of a "thin theory of the self." This is a self that is thin precisely because it has been stripped of those subjective properties of self-understanding so dreaded under the natural science model. It is a thin self because it is a self disengaged from the deeply held commitments that the drive to neutrality must reject. It is a view of the self, says Taylor, that has a powerful hold on us for primarily two reasons. The first is that it is compatible with a study of human behavior modeled on the natural sciences. This view of the self thus gets a sort of prestige by association. The impressive accomplishments of the natural science model in understanding the world of nature is held out, and a promise of similar explanatory feats is offered for the obliging social scientist.

The second motivation for adopting this thin theory of the self is even more powerful. This motivation derives from the fact that the picture of the agent that lies behind this view of the self is an extraordinarily attractive one in the modern world. It is a picture of an agent who is free and utterly autonomous. It is a picture of an agent who can achieve a disengagement from the world by objectifying it, who creates rather than discovers his purposes, and who views the world as a sort of empty stage upon which the posited values are pursued (HAL, 4). Such a view of human agency, Taylor notes, is "flattering and inspiring." It gives us a sense of dignity, power, and imperturbability. It is also deeply misleading.

One of the ways in which such a view of agency is most deceptive is in the conception of freedom it offers. It is the freedom of the "self-defining subject." It is a freedom in which the agent is capable of radical choice. On this view, agents can choose their most basic values, loyalties, and aspirations independently of, and unconstrained by, the interference of others.

The self-defining subject chooses his identity by choosing his purposes and goals out of himself. There is here an "inner horizon" of value and identity (PHS, 258), and the upshot is that the agent is understood to be "metaphysically independent of society" (HAL, 8). The freedom of the self-defining subject is thus also the freedom of the atomistic self. Unfortunately, both distort the reality of human life.

By this point, it should be clear that the thin theory of the self is more or less the same view that we previously identified as the emotivist self. We have already seen that such a view of the self is wholly inadequate. But what is the alternative here? The alternative view emerges through a study of human behavior modeled, not on the natural sciences, but on the insights of hermeneutics. It takes as its starting point precisely what the natural science model is committed to rejecting, namely, the centrality of self-interpretation to any understanding of human life and action. According to the hermeneutical view, it is not possible to adequately understand human behavior without reference to the agent's understanding of his or her actions for we are fundamentally "self-interpreting animals."

This means that it is not possible to view human behavior from a detached and neutral standpoint because our sense of ourselves and our situations is at least partly constitutive of who we are. To seek to eliminate this interpretation of ourselves and our experience in order to maintain detachment and neutrality is thus to move farther from, rather than closer to, an adequate understanding of human behavior (HAL, 47).

Moreover, since our self-understanding is essentially evaluative, since, that is, we interpret ourselves and our lives against a background of "distinctions of worth," our very identities are defined by certain evaluations (HAL, 34). From this perspective, therefore, the attempt to understand human life according to the natural science model is hopelessly doomed to fail for a natural science model inevitably seeks to eliminate evaluative judgments; it seeks neutrality. Yet, human behavior cannot be studied like the human body. We can understand the workings of a bodily organ like the heart without reference to the beliefs and judgments of the person whose heart we are studying. An echocardiogram requires no investigation of self-understanding. But we cannot understand the behavior of someone whose "heart" is broken without reference to how the person whose "heart" it is understands his or her situation (HAL, 3-4).

The inevitable failure of the natural science model might not be so troubling if this approach did not continue to exert such an influence on our understanding of human agency and self-hood, but it does. The thin theory of the self that accompanies this view, its vision of the radically free agent, and its atomistic understanding of human life, all hide from us "the way in which an individual is constituted by the language and culture which can only be maintained and renewed in the communities he is part of" (HAL, 8).

Indeed, I think it is plausible to argue, although Taylor does not argue this, that what is fundamentally at stake between these two approaches to the study of human behavior is the view of freedom articulated by each approach and the corresponding understanding of human agency. We have already seen that, on the natural science model, freedom is understood as absolute. Freedom on this view is a Sartrean freedom, where the agent is continually confronted by situations of radical choice. On this view, the agent is indeed condemned to be free, for at every moment the individual is free to redefine the world in terms of his or her wishes. In contrast, on the hermeneutical view, human freedom is a bounded freedom. On the hermeneutical view, the very notion of radical freedom is incoherent.

Taylor makes this point in connection to the famous example of Sartre's student who, during the second world war, is torn between caring for his aging and ill mother and joining the Resistance to fight for his country. In Sartre's account, the choice facing this young man is illustrative of the human situation generally. One is confronted with a choice for which there are no criteria; one is totally free to choose, because there is no way of adjudicating between these competing claims. As Taylor points out, however, the reader perceives this as a moral dilemma precisely because he or she acknowledges that there are rival claims here, that there are values which are binding in this case regardless of what or how we choose. In other words, Sartre is able to portray this situation as one of radical choice only by introducing rival moral claims, which themselves could not be created by radical choice. If one is truly free to ignore the claims of one's ailing mother or one's country, there is no dilemma here at all.

This means, of course, that the notions of radical freedom and radical choice are illusory. So, too, is the view of agency that goes with these. We are not agents capable of stepping back totally from our "horizons of value" and choosing. There is no Kantian transcendental subject given prior to its ends. Neither is the self primarily constituted by the ends it chooses. This is why the view of moral deliberation embedded in the natural science model is so misleading. Whether it results in a deontological view or in an utilitarian one, the primary conceptualization is that of self-as-chooser. Yet, in the hermeneutical view the proper conceptualization is rather self-as-discoverer for in the hermeneutical view to be a self "is to exist in a space defined by distinctions of worth" (HAL, 3). To be a self, to have an identity, is to have already a horizon of value out of which one evaluates and chooses. This means that our central values are at least partly discovered, not chosen, for we always find ourselves already choosing within a horizon of value. This is precisely what the theory of radical choice seeks to escape, and what makes it incoherent. According to Taylor:

> The agent of radical choice would at the moment of choice have *ex hypothesi*, no horizon of evaluation. He would be utterly without identity. He would be

a kind of extensionless point, a pure leap into the void. But such a thing is an impossibility, or rather could only be the description of the most terrible mental alienation. The subject of radical choice is another avatar of that recurrent figure which our civilization aspires to realize, the disembodied ego, the subject who can objectify all being, including his own, and choose in radical freedom. But this promised total self-possession would in fact be the most total self-loss. (HAL, 35)

This picture of unlimited freedom obscures just how dependent we are on language and culture for we discover our horizons of value in communities of which we are inescapably a part. The community is constitutive of the individual because the self-interpretations that form the identities of selves are inevitably mediated through communal belief and practice.

Saying that we are constituted in community through the distinctions of worth provided by language, however, does not mean we are incapable of choice. On the contrary, we would be incapable of choice without these background distinctions. It means instead that we can never completely detach ourselves from these background conditions. We can reflect on these distinctions of worth, we can gain some perspective on them, but we cannot escape them. Michael Sandel has captured the sense of this bounded freedom:

> To imagine a person incapable of constitutive attachments such as these is not to conceive an ideally free and rational agent, but to imagine a person wholly without character, without moral depth. For to have character is to know that I move in a history I neither summon nor command, which carries consequences none the less for my choices and conduct. . . . As a self-interpreting being, I am able to reflect on my history and in this sense distance myself from it, but the distance is always precarious and provisional, the point of reflection never finally secured outside the history itself. A person with character thus knows that he is implicated in various ways even as he reflects, and feels the moral weight of what he knows.[2]

Feeling the moral weight of what we know need not leave us paralyzed. We can acknowledge that our evaluations are not, for the most part, chosen and nevertheless seek to ensure that they are not totally arbitrary either. We can acknowledge, in other words, that we live in a world of meanings that we do not perfectly understand, and that our task is to try to interpret these meanings as best we can (HAL, 112). The important point, the one lost sight of when human action is approached according to the natural science model, is that these meanings and interpretations are inextricably embedded in community.

The Recovery of Self-Understanding I

We can appreciate at this point just how powerfully a recognition of the baleful effects of a natural science paradigm to our understanding of moral agency complements our previous emphasis on the importance of narrative. Recall that I argued in the first chapter that the problem with contemporary moral philosophy is that it adopts a scientific paradigm of objectivity, which in turn leads it to adopt the standard account of moral rationality. The trouble with the standard account is that it truncates moral experience in a way that eliminates the possibility of understanding how Christian convictions shape lives. The underlying difficulty, we saw, was that the standard account necessarily assumes an abstract conception of the self.

We can now see more precisely what is mistaken about such a view, namely, it prescinds from the importance of self-understanding in the moral life, and all that self-understanding entails. One consequence of ignoring the role of self-understanding is the distortion of the nature of human agency. We do not exist in unbounded freedom, nor are we metaphysically independent of society. The mistake of thinking that we are is not simply the result of epistemological preoccupations but more directly the consequence of a certain moral self-understanding that values power, dignity, and self-control. Yet, if we are to overcome this inadequate account of moral agency, we need more than an epistemological critique—we need a change in self-understanding.

It is in this context that we can appreciate the full significance of our previous discussion of character, vision, and narrative. These three themes offer an alternative self-understanding. In essence, what Hauerwas offers is an alternative way of understanding oneself. Especially in his discussion of the place of narrative in the moral life, Hauerwas is urging his readers to abandon the Olympian ideal of control that is offered by the standard account. In its place, he puts a vision of humility engendered by a sense that we are but one part in a much larger narrative, that we are as dependent on others as on ourselves for our sense of self-identity, and that this is how it should be. This is why Hauerwas says that freedom "is not a name for some real or ideal state in which we have absolute control of our lives."[3] The truly essential connection here is not between freedom and agency but between agency and narrative. The "power of any agency depends exactly on the adequacy of the descriptions we learn from our communities," and these descriptions are communicated via the narratives of particular communities (PK, 43). We do not exist in unbounded freedom, but are crucially dependent on the communities of which we are a part, communities that play a role in shaping our lives through the narratives they offer us.

Unfortunately, we lose sight of, or perhaps refuse to see, our boundedness when we adopt a scientific paradigm for understanding the moral life. Such a paradigm inevitably seeks control in a way that easily leads to a kind of hubris, one manifestation of which is the illusion that we are totally in control of our lives, and that all moral disagreements can satisfactorily be adjudicated. What significance do these two insights have to the present study? One answer is simply this: positing an ideal of control precludes the emotions from serious consideration within the moral life because emotions are experiences over which we do not have total control. We have already seen how the urge for control can eclipse emotions, for it is this concern for control that underlies the Kantian quest for moral self-sufficiency. Once again, then, we encounter the dynamic by which emotions are relegated to the periphery of the moral life. The drive to objectivity and the urge to neutrality and disengagement will at the same time be a movement to push emotions off the stage.

If the quest for objectivity is indeed a quest for control, then our emotions are bound to appear problematic for we do not summon our emotions at will, nor do we appear completely free to choose our emotions. To allow our emotions an important place in the moral life will thus run seriously afoul of the conception of the self offered by the objectivist approach. The self-as-chooser cannot afford the emotions a prominent place because we do not choose our emotions. The "significance free" conception of personhood, that view of the self that seeks to understand the self apart from the ends and goals that are significant to the individual, will always seek to leave behind human emotions. The unbounded freedom that this view seeks aspires "to rise above the merely human, to step outside the prison of the peculiarly human emotions, and to be free of the cares and the demands they make on us" (HAL, 112). To this view, human emotions will always appear to be a prison simply because they do express our cares and they do make demands on us. Notice, too, that emotions are not being rejected on this view because they are considered insignificant by individuals who are actually trying to live morally. On the contrary, the fact that emotions do play a role is precisely the problem. Rather, emotions are dismissed on this view because they do not fit easily into the canonical account of the moral life as controlled and rationalistic.

The explanation of why emotions have been ignored in recent moral theory, which emerges from reflecting on the nature of moral agency, is thus closer to the second of the two explanations offered above. Emotions have been marginalized in contemporary moral theory as a result of epistemological preoccupations. The obsessive concern for foundations has in general worked to eliminate emotions from serious consideration in the moral life, but perhaps an even more powerful force for eliminating emotions has been the drive for control in the moral life. The vision of unbounded freedom and control is indeed attractive; unfortunately, there is no room in this vision for a rich and substantial emotional life. Again, note that the reasons for scorning emotions are not, on either view, dictated by reflection on the lived experience of moral agents, but by methodological presuppositions.

There is a second way in which the significance of control to the natural science model is relevant to our study, and it is one that allows us to see exactly how important a hermeneutical view is to accounting for the place of the emotions in the moral life. We have seen that approaching the study of human behavior according to the natural science model involves an attempt to understand human life from outside, so to speak, a neutral and detached point of view. One implication of this approach is that the self gets treated as simply one object among others, a perspective from which self-interpretation or self-understanding is unimportant. We have also seen that such a conception of the self, and its corresponding conception of freedom, cannot do justice to the way in which we ordinarily deliberate and choose from within a horizon of value. Yet just as we cannot think of the self in this detached or disengaged way, if we are going to make sense of the experience of human choice, so, too, we cannot think of the self in this way if we are going to make sense of human emotions. Emotions involve a fundamental sense of ourselves and our situations and thus become unintelligible in a context where this sense of self is stripped away. In other words, when self-understanding is thought to be unimportant, emotions will become mysterious. It is worth looking at this claim in some detail.

At the heart of this conception of the relation between self-understanding and emotions is the claim that emotions involve a sense of ourselves and our situations. Consider, for example, the emotion of shame. We can begin by asking the question: What makes a particular feeling one of shame? The answer is that shame is a feeling essentially connected to a sense that I have done something dishonorable, or that there is something about myself that I would like to hide. I feel shame when I believe that I am responsible for something that brings discredit on me.[4] In other words, a feeling is one of shame when I am concerned that I have failed to meet some standard, a standard that I have an aspiration to meet. "To experience an emotion is to be in a sense struck or moved by our situation being of a certain nature" (HAL, 107). In the case of shame we are struck or moved by the sense that our situation is a shameful or humiliating one, and we are moved precisely because we do not care to be humiliated.

Now if this is a correct account of the nature of our emotions—and I will argue in the next chapter that it is—we can see why the objectivist view of the self will wish to downplay the significance of the emotions. The objectivist account seeks to understand human life from an absolute perspective. It thus seeks to understand human actions from a neutral and detached perspective; it seeks to redescribe the experiences of human life without reference to how the subject of those experiences actually experiences them. But if emotions necessarily incorporate a sense of ourselves and our situations, this is precisely what cannot be done. To attempt fully to account for emotions without consideration of subjective experience is thus like trying to describe a home but instead sketching a house: One may capture some of the external structure, but the central features are missing.

The hope that it might be possible to give an absolute or objectivist account of emotions is fueled by the fact that in the case of some emotions, it does seem possible to give a coherent account of the emotion that makes no reference to how the subject experiences it. Take the example of physical fear. It might be possible to describe the experience of physical fear in a way that explained the relationship between situation and response without appealing to experience-dependent properties; that is, it appears possible to characterize the significance of a situation of physical danger independently of an individual's experience of that danger. For example, it is possible to characterize the significance of a dangerous situation in medical terms, as, say, threatening certain life-sustaining physiological processes. The fact that a fall from a certain height will be fatal is a "culture-resistant" fact which can be characterized independently of an individual's interpretation of that fact.

Still, even here the objectivist account, while coherent, does not capture the significance of physical danger to me. If I fear a disease that threatens certain life-sustaining physiological processes of mine, the object of my fear is not even remotely captured by a description of this disease process such as might be found, say, in a medical textbook. What I fear is the disease that may take away my life.[5] This fear cannot be adequately described in experience-independent terms. It was this truth that Tolstoy, for example, captured in his story, *The Death of Ivan Ilyich*. Ivan, seeing his imminent death, reflects on the possibility of understanding it from a distance:

> The syllogism he had learned from Kiesewetter's logic—"Caius is a man, men are mortal, therefore Caius is mortal"—had always seemed to him correct as applied to Caius, but by no means to himself. That Caius represented man in the abstract, and so the reasoning was perfectly sound; but he was not Caius, not an abstract man; he had always been a creature quite, quite distinct from all the others. He had been little Vanya with a mama and a papa . . . Vanya, with all the joys, sorrows, and enthusiasms of his childhood, boyhood, and youth. Had Caius ever known the smell of that little striped leather ball Vanya had loved so much? Had Caius ever kissed his mother's hand so dearly, and had the silk folds of her dress ever rustled so for him?[6]

The point, of course, is that it is not possible to understand this fear from a distance. Ivan's fear is constituted in relation to that which he holds closest to his heart and which is at risk. Consequently, an experience-independent account of Ivan's fear of death is simply not possible.

Even if a completely objectivist account could be given of physical fear, it does not follow that such an account can be given of other, more complex human emotions. It cannot, for example, be given of shame. Since this point is of such importance, it is worth quoting Taylor at some length here. "Shame," he says,

> is an emotion that a subject experiences in relation to a dimension of his existence as a subject. What we can be ashamed of are properties which are essentially properties of a subject. This may not be immediately evident, because I may be ashamed of my shrill voice, or my effeminate hands. But of course it only makes sense to see these as objects of shame if they have for me or my culture an expressive dimension: a shrill voice is (to me, to my culture) something unmanly, betokens hysteria, not something solid, strong, macho, self-contained. It does not radiate a sense of strength, capacity, superiority. Effeminate hands are—effeminate. Both voice and hands clash with what I aspire to be, feel that my dignity demands that I be, as a person, a presence among others. (HAL, 53)

Taylor's point is that it is not possible to give an account of shame which does not make essential reference to how the individual experiences his or her situation. What is considered shameful is not, as in the case of what is physically dangerous, a culture-resistant fact. That certain properties, such as a shrill voice and effeminate hands, are demeaning is true only for a subject who understands these properties to have this meaning. For this reason, it is not possible to give an experience-independent account of shame. Indeed, says Taylor "the very account of what shame means involves reference to things—like our sense of dignity, of worth, of how we are seen by others—which are essentially bound up with the life of a subject of experience" (HAL, 54). Shame, and many other emotions like it, necessarily incorporate a sense of self-understanding in relation to the situations in which we find ourselves.

The example of shame thus displays the important connection between a hermeneutical view of the self and human emotions. In fact, I believe it would not be too strong to say that the very idea that we are self-interpreting beings, that self-understanding must be at the center of any fruitful understanding of human life, requires that emotions be given a prominent place in that life. We can see this point by considering the fact that the place where the role of self-interpretation manifests itself most transparently in human life is in our emotions. As we have seen, our emotions depend on the import things have for us and what import things have for us is dependent on our interpretations of ourselves and our situations. In other words, because our emotions are essentially constituted by our self-understanding, the evaluations, desires, and aspirations that make up that self-understanding will be woven into our emotional lives (HAL, 68). It follows from this that we will not be able fully to account for self-understanding without reference to emotions, or our emotions without reference to self-understanding. Indeed, we can now see how emotions become an important source of self-revelation, for they disclose to us those things about ourselves and our situations that we truly value. This is why it makes sense to say that our "subject-referring" emotions, "open us on to the domain of what it is to be human" (HAL, 62), by which Taylor means that emotions make manifest to us what matters most to us *qua* subjects of experience. To say that we are self-interpreting beings, it turns out, is to say that we are beings "whose emotional life incorporates a sense of what is really important to him" (HAL, 74).

Language, Culture, and Emotional Transformation

At this point, we must take with us several important conclusions. We must acknowledge the intimate relationship between an understanding of human agency and our assessment of the significance of human emotions. We must keep in mind that, on the one hand, to embrace an objectivist view of agency is likely to eliminate human emotions as morally significant and, on the other hand, to assign emotions a prominent place in the moral life we must do justice to the way in which our agency is shaped by our understanding of ourselves and our situations. This, in turn, leads us to an equally important observation: we can make sense of our emotions only if we acknowledge the extent to which they are embedded in a language and a culture.

This cultural embeddedness of human emotions emerges simply as an extrapolation of our affirmation that emotions incorporate a sense of our situation as being of a certain sort. We can only understand a situation as being of a certain type linguistically. This is why Taylor says that emotions incorporate an "articulation" of our situation and why saying that emotions are constituted by our self-understanding is more or less equivalent to saying that emotions are constituted by language. We can see this point in connection with our previous discussion of shame. We discovered in this earlier discussion that the emotion of shame incorporates a sense of our situation as humiliating or dishonorable or the like. Shame thus presupposes that we are capable of characterizing our situation in these or similar terms. But if this is the case, it begins to appear that in order even to experience the emotion of shame, we must have a vocabulary or lexicon that includes such contrasting terms as "worthy/unworthy," "honorable/dishonorable," "dignified/undignified." Moreover, the mere existence of such a lexicon is not enough; we must also understand the "experiential meaning" of our emotional vocabulary. In order to understand the concepts necessary to the experience of shame, we must have a feel, so to speak, for the language and action of blame, admiration, etc. (PHS, 24). In other words, the emotion of shame is embedded in a social practice that is circumscribed by an evaluative language of admiration and blame.[7]

We will return to this point in a moment. For now, it is important to be clear about how essential language is to the formation of our emotional life. We can bring this point into sharper focus if we consider how even our prearticulate emotional experiences are not language independent, and how the process of clarifying an inarticulate emotion involves giving definition to the experience, thereby shaping the experience through the use of language.

Consider first the experience of an inarticulate emotion. This is certainly a common enough experience: we feel troubled or disturbed, or perhaps we experience a nameless anxiety. It has sometimes been suggested that these experiences demonstrate that emotions are language independent. At first blush, this appears to be the appropriate conclusion to draw. A closer examination, however, indicates that these examples do not demonstrate this at all, for, in both cases, the emotional experiences are still crucially shaped by the individual's sense of his or her situation. In the case of a feeling that we cannot quite name, it is constitutive of the experience that we experience it as perplexing (HAL, 74).[8] Similarly, in the case of nameless anxiety, it does not follow that because we cannot identify the source of our anxiety, that this experience is linguistically unstructured. We clearly have a sense of dread or fear, even if we cannot say of what (HAL, 48).

If we attend to the process of clarifying an emotional experience, the centrality of the role of language becomes even more transparent. Suppose, for example, that I am troubled by a movie that I have just seen. Although I am somewhat confused about my feelings about the movie, when asked, I simply report that I did not like it. My emotional response to the movie may remain at this relatively inarticulate level or it may be developed and clarified. If, for example, I am pressed to say what I did not like about the movie, I may come to see that what is really troubling me is the grossly insensitive and stereotypical way in which homosexuality is depicted in the film. If I am now asked what it is about the film that I do not like, I will respond that I find the portrayal of homosexuality in the film objectionable, and that I believe the filmmakers repeatedly appealed to the baser instincts of the audience merely to elicit a few cheap laughs. If I respond in this way, I may well discover that my feelings are no longer confused. Where before, my emotional reaction was a vague, negative one, it may now be quite clear: I am angry and indignant. In other words, my emotional response has been clarified through the process of articulating my sense of the situation.

What begins to emerge at this point is how closely allied are the three themes on which we have placed such emphasis: the centrality of self-understanding, the constitutive role of language, and the significance of emotions in human life. The connection between self-understanding and emotions we have already explored. We can now appreciate how these three themes really come together in terms of a particular understanding of the nature of human language. Once again, how one approaches human behavior, in this case the use of language, is dictated by whether one adopts a natural science model or a hermeneutical one. If a natural science model is followed, one will likely embrace a "designative" theory of language. On a designative view, language is understood primarily as an "instrument of control in gaining knowledge of the world as objective process" (HAL, 226). On this view, language serves primarily to describe or depict the world and meaning is understood in terms of the relation of linguistic reality to extralinguistic reality.[9]

By contrast, if one adopts a hermeneutical approach to the study of language, an "expressive" theory is the more likely result. An expressive theory of language abandons the preoccupation with control and consequently runs counter to the scientific quest for objectivity. On the expressive theory, language does not function primarily to depict objective reality, but to express or manifest meaning. And meaning cannot be understood by mapping language to bits of extralinguistic reality but only by reference to other linguistic expressions.

The designative and expressive theories will disagree about whether language is an activity essentially bound to a community. Both theories will agree that we learn language in a community, but on the designative view, it makes sense to talk of an individual maintaining a sort of private monologue once a language is learned. This is because meaning is not understood to be largely a matter of intersubjective agreement, but of correspondence between language and reality. In contrast, on the expressive view, one of the essential functions of language is the creation of a "public space," within which the use of language always takes place. As Taylor puts it, "language serves to place some matter out in the open between interlocutors" (HAL, 259). It creates a space of intersubjective meaning in which we come to understand our world.

We see here that an expressive view of language offers a sort of cement for binding together the accounts of self-understanding, community, and emotion that I have just articulated for on an expressive view, language is largely constitutive of self, community, and emotion. As a symbolic medium that expresses a way of being in the world, language is the vehicle by which we come to understand ourselves and our community as well as to have proper human emotions (HAL, 234).

In one sense, of course, by highlighting the constitutive role of language, we simply draw attention to the powerful role language can play in the process of personal conversion, whether religious or otherwise. The ability to redescribe the world is the power fundamentally to alter how one feels about oneself and the world. This, too, is an idea beautifully rendered by Tolstoy in *The Death of Ivan Ilyich:*

> And in his imagination he [Ivan] called to mind the best moments of his pleasant life. Yet, strangely enough, all the best moments of his pleasant life now

seemed entirely different than they had in the past—all except the earliest memories of childhood. Way back in his childhood there had been something really pleasant, something he could live with were it ever to recur. *But the person who had experienced that happiness no longer existed. It was as though he were recalling the memories of another man.*

As soon as he got to the period that had produced the present Ivan Ilyich, all the seeming joys of his life vanished before his sight and turned into something trivial and often nasty.¹⁰

Here, then, we see how a hermeneutical understanding of the self and an expressive theory of language come together to produce a powerful explanatory framework for understanding the potential of religious belief and practice to transform our lives by transforming our emotions. This framework allows us to account for the way in which, like Ivan, our emotions may be changed by coming to accept a new self-understanding and with it a new moral and emotional vocabulary.

If we pause now to reflect on how thoroughly religious belief and practice may shape one's self-understanding, we begin to get a glimmer of how important religious faith can be to the emotional life of the believer for religious belief and practice can provide the vocabulary for transforming both self-understanding and our views about everyday existence. And, as we have just seen, such transformations can shape one's emotional life. Indeed, if we return to Taylor one final time, we see this point forcefully articulated. Taylor writes:

> If we are partly constituted by our self-understanding, and this in turn can be very different according to the various languages which articulate for us a background of distinctions of worth, then language does not only serve to depict ourselves and the world, it also helps constitute our lives. Certain ways of being, of feeling, of relating to each other are only possible given certain linguistic resources. Without a certain articulation of oneself and of the highest, it is neither possible to be a Christian ascetic nor to feel that combination of one's own lack of worth and high calling (the "grandeur et misere" of Pascal), nor to be part of, say, a monastic order. (HAL, 9–10)

Religious belief and practice, in other words, may provide the necessary community of discourse to sustain certain ways of being and feeling.

This is essentially the point we acknowledged earlier when we observed that Christian narratives may help to form our affections by answering the question: Who am I? By stressing the importance of narrative in the moral life, we become alive to the capacity of religious faith to shape self-understanding in fundamental ways. Further, this conception of the role of narrative also opens to view the role religious faith can play in forming our emotions. By answering the question, "Who am I?" Christian narratives provide the categories of self-understanding, the moral vocabularies that generate and support particular emotions. In this case, Christian belief and practice provide a form of life in which particular emotions flourish and others wither.

We can see, then, that in order to account for the importance of religious faith in the moral life we must understand how faith can transform the whole person and that religious narratives may play an important role in this process. Further, we can now appreciate, at least in outline form, how a religious transformation of emotions is possible and why it is important. As we have seen, it is possible because our emotions are constituted by our self-understandings and crucially depend on our articulations of ourselves and our situations. Since religious belief may provide the categories in which this self-understanding is articulated, it may dramatically shape our emotions. Accounting for this sort of transformation is important because our emotions are so central to the moral life. That emotions are indeed central becomes clear once we abandon a natural science approach to the study of morality. Indeed, once we jettison objectivist pretensions, we arrive at a model of practical deliberation according to which it is a failure of reason *not* to rely on emotions when deliberating morally. Emotions are thus returned to their rightful place at the heart of the moral life and the possibility of moral growth through emotion transformation comes into view.

The remainder of this study is devoted to examining the possibility of this sort of transformation in more detail. We can begin this examination with a closer look at Taylor's claim that emotions are constituted by a sense of ourselves and our situations. As we have seen, it is this claim, and the suggestion implicit in this claim—that emotions are constituted by beliefs and judgments—that frames the possibility of accounting for how religious faith shapes our emotions. We thus turn in the next chapter to a more sustained discussion of the claim that emotions are cognitively structured.

3

Toward a Constructivist
Theory of Emotion

When we turn to consider the claim that emotions are partly constituted by our sense of ourselves and our situation, we once again confront an obstacle erected by the attempt to understand human behavior according to a model taken from the natural sciences. We have seen how, in general, the quest for an objectivist account of human life has obscured the importance of self-understanding, and this is no less true in the particular case of the study of human emotions. We face a double barrier here. On the one hand, emotions have for so long been treated as essentially irrational and uncontrollable that there is a strong presumption against any theory of emotion which seeks to challenge this picture. On the other hand, the attempt to study emotions "scientifically" has generally involved an attempt to understand emotions independently of self-understanding, and when emotions are so construed, they cannot but appear irrational and uncontrollable.

To overcome these barriers we need to answer two questions: (1) Why have emotions been understood to be independent of the judgments and beliefs characteristic of self-understanding? and (2) Is there a plausible alternative here? In other words, is there a theory of emotions that will accommodate a constitutive role for self-understanding? Let us consider these questions in turn.

The Absence of Self-Understanding on the Traditional View

The view that self-understanding has no significant role in our emotional lives has often been called a "noncognitivist" view of emotion, and we can begin to appreciate the appeal of such a theory by considering one of the most famous noncognitive theories of emotion, that espoused by William

James.[1] James has played a critical role in contemporary psychology of religion, and he is important to us for a number of reasons. First, James's emphasis on the centrality of human affections in religious life has been enormously influential. Second, his account of human emotion is a paradigmatic example of a theory that obscures the importance of self-understanding. The combination of these two facts presents an irony. James's argument for the importance of affective experience makes our insistence on the centrality of emotions in the moral life more credible, while, at the same time, his noncognitive theory of emotions makes it more difficult to account for how religious life can in fact shape our emotions. It is worth briefly exploring this irony.

The claim that emotions are the heart of religious life is found in James's book, *The Varieties of Religious Experience*. In the second to the last chapter of this work, James makes an intriguing comment about emotions that helps explain both how James understood emotions to be central to religious life and why his understanding of emotions makes it so difficult to appreciate how religious life can transform our emotions. He tells his audience that he plans to defend the view that religion is an "essentially private and individualistic" affair which is based on human affections. "I do believe," he writes, "that feeling is the deeper source of religion, and that philosophic and theological formulas are secondary products, *like translations of a text* into another tongue."[2] This remark comes at the beginning of a chapter on the relation of philosophy to religious experience, and the metaphor of emotion as text that James invokes here is meant to symbolize what he sees as the secondary and derivative status of philosophy in relation to faith. What is of fundamental importance, what is central, is the private affective experience of the individual. The attempt to understand or to justify one's faith is secondary. This is what the image of emotion as text is meant to convey. Just as a text is that which a reader must interpret and explain, so is private emotional experience that which philosophers and theologians must decipher. Just as a text has primacy, so too does affective religious experience.[3]

One of the reasons that James appeals here to the primacy of religious affections is to protect religion from the corrosive effects of modern science. James was fully aware that in a period where the traditional category of authority as a standard of truth has given way to a modern conception of probability as a standard of truth, any emphasis on the content of religious beliefs or on the metaphysical commitments of one's faith is likely to highlight the tenuous cognitive status of religious life.[4] By contrast, if we say, with James, that religious affections have primacy, if we say that philosophical and theological formulas are ultimately unnecessary accretions, then religious life would appear to be fortified against the dangers that threaten it from evidential standards of truth. On this view, proof would seem to depend on the experience itself, and the individual has privileged access to his own experience. Appeals to affective religious experience as the core of religious life thus appear to make religion invulnerable to the challenges of modern science.[5]

Yet, even here, where James offers a particularly alluring account of the importance of religious affections, we see the contrast that poses such problems for an effort to understand how religious life may transform our emotions, on the one hand, belief and cognition on the other. This contrast emerges even more clearly when we turn to James's explicit discussion of the nature of human emotion. According to the so-called James-Lange theory, an emotion is simply the feeling one has when undergoing physiological changes in response to external stimuli. "Our natural way of thinking about these standard emotions," James writes,

> is that the mental perception of some fact excites the mental affection called the emotion, and that this latter state of mind gives rise to the bodily expression. My thesis on the contrary is that the bodily changes follow directly the PERCEPTION of the exciting fact, and that our feeling of the same changes as they occur IS the emotion.[6]

For James, emotions are essentially sensations; we feel our bodies responding to certain stimuli, and this feeling is itself the emotion. As James himself points out, this way of putting the matter is a bit odd for it has the peculiar consequence of reversing what we normally take the sequence of events here to be. As James put it, in his view we do not cry because we are sorry, we are sorry because we cry. That is, we do not manifest physiological changes as the result of experiencing an emotion, rather it is our experience of a physiological change that is the emotion. Why does James embrace a theory that appears so counterintuitive, and why has his theory been so influential in the twentieth century?

The answers to both questions are found in the fact that the theory allows one to approach the study of human emotions according to a natural science methodology. Recall that this approach involves abstracting from the subjective experiences of individuals in order to give an "absolute" account of human behavior in experience-independent terms. This is precisely what James's theory attempts, for he defines emotions in such a way that they are, in principle, identifiable independently of the subjective experiences of agents. This may not at first be obvious because James in fact says that it is our feeling of bodily changes that is the emotion. But James also makes it clear that these essentially private feelings are mediated by physiological structures that are, in principle, public and therefore intersubjectively univocal.

Moreover, it is quite clear that James intended his theory to make the study of emotions "scientific." In the Preface to his *Principles of Psychology*, for example, he explicitly acknowledges that he is attempting to develop a "natural science of psychology." Nowhere is this effort more in evidence than in his chapter on the emotions for it is in this chapter that two of James's fascinations with science come together: on the one hand his interest in the development of the brain and the workings of the nervous system, and on the other his interest in Darwin's account of the physiological expression of emotion in humans and other animals.[7] Thus, I think Robert Solomon is correct when he suggests that James saw the science of neurology as a possible foundation for a scientific psychology and that, consequently, in James's work "the application of the new concepts of neurophysiology to the psychology of the emotions was direct and unhesitating"[8]

Undoubtedly, then, one reason why James is attracted to a noncognitive view of emotions is that such a view appears sufficiently scientific. No doubt, too, it is partially this fact that explains why James's theory has been so influential. By combining the concepts of neurophysiology with an emphasis on the feelings characteristic of particular emotions, James simultaneously provided a scientifically credible version of the traditional view that emotions are feelings[9] and provided for psychologists a bailiwick with respect to emotions that they could call their own, namely, the investigation of the underlying neurophysiological structure of emotion. One answer to our question about why emotions have been considered to be independent of judgment and belief, therefore, is that such a view effectively severs the ties between emotions and subjective experience and thus frees emotions to be the appropriate objects of scientific investigation. A noncognitive view thus offers the promise of an objective account of human emotions in which emotions could be explained, without loss, in terms that are experience-independent and intersubjectively verifiable. This, in any event, was certainly the goal of those psychologists who followed James and vigorously sought to identify distinct physiological states associated with particular emotions.[10]

Consider the consequences of adopting a noncognitive view of emotions. Among other things, embracing a noncognitive theory leads to the assimilation of emotions to sensations, to a passive and mechanistic understanding of emotional behavior, and to a sharp dichotomy between reason and emotion. We find all of these in James's account. James says, for example, that the neurological structures that mediate human emotions are little more than a "hyphen" between external stimuli in the world and genetically predetermined responses of our bodies to those stimuli. He writes:

> The love of man for woman, or of the human mother for her babe, our wrath at snakes, or our fear of precipices, may all be described similarly as instances of the way in which peculiarly conformed pieces of the world's furniture will fatal-

ly call forth most particular mental and bodily reactions, in advance of, and often in direct opposition to, the verdict of our deliberate reason concerning them.[11]

James's view is here representative of most noncognitive views, according to which emotions are essentially reducible to sensations. To treat emotions as sensations does not, of course, allow much room for discussing the role of self-understanding in emotional experience, but it does allow emotions to be treated "scientifically."

So we see an answer to our first question concerning why emotions have been treated as noncognitive. Is an alternative theory of emotion available? What sort of theory would, in contrast with a noncognitive theory, afford self-understanding a prominent place in shaping human emotions? We can perhaps begin to distinguish an alternative perspective on human emotions by identifying two differentia that help us distinguish those theories which will provide for self-understanding from those that will seek its elimination. If, in contrast with the noncognitive view, we label those theories that provide a place for self-understanding "cognitive" theories of emotion, we may state the distinction as follows. A cognitive theory, in contrast with a noncognitive one, makes an individual's sense of his or her situation: (1) a constitutive feature of the concept of an emotion; and (2) necessary for individuating particular emotions.[12]

Stating the distinction in these terms makes it clear that James's theory is indeed a noncognitive one because there is no room for individual appraisal on James's account. Even from our brief sketch we can see, for example, that for James beliefs and judgments have no place among the defining characteristics of an emotion. On the contrary, the emotion is just the feeling of bodily changes, and these changes are themselves only reflex bodily effects produced by environmental cues. Nor, for James, are emotions individuated by appeal to the appropriate cognitions. Rather, emotions are distinguished, one from another, through introspection: looking within, one identifies a certain feeling as that associated with anger, say, rather than with fear.

Problems with the Traditional View

We can see both why we need to move toward a cognitive account of emotion and what such an account would look like by attending to some of the difficulties posed for a theory that eliminates any reference to self-understanding from the defining characteristics of emotions. We have already seen how important belief and judgment are in emotional experience. We saw, for example, that the emotion of shame incorporates a belief that there is something about myself that I wish to hide. If I am ashamed, I have a sense of my situation as being humiliating or shameful, and this sense does not appear incidental. Unfortunately, this is precisely that for which the noncognitive theory cannot account because on the noncognitive theory there is no essential relation between emotion and cognition.

Philosophers have sometimes put this point by saying that a noncognitive theory cannot account for the "intentional" character of emotions, that is, emotions are almost always about something.[13] We are rarely, if ever, simply angry, proud, or afraid. Rather we are angry *at* someone, proud *of* something, afraid *of* something or someone. Yet, if anger, say, is always anger about something, then anger will include reference to belief and judgment in a way that feeling or sensation does not. We do not ask about the object of a stomach ache or about that of fatigue, but we do ask about the object of anger. And when we ask about the object of anger, we are asking about the beliefs or judgments that make anger an appropriate response in a particular situation. We expect an answer of the following sort: "I'm angry with Michael because he insulted me during the meeting." In this case, my anger includes a cognitive appraisal that Michael said something to or about me during the meeting that was insulting.

Unfortunately, because a noncognitive theory severs the connection between emotions and our sense of our situation, it cannot provide a place for questions about the objects of our emotions. It thus collapses the distinction between emotions and mere sensation. Indeed, we can see that James's account is reduced to a point of absurdity on this score for on James's account it is impossible to distinguish a state produced by chemical injection from an emotion brought about by coming across a hungry bear in the woods. The fact that the first state is not about anything, that it is unconnected to beliefs about the presence of danger, for example, is irrelevant on James's account. Because, for James, emotions are merely the feelings of bodily changes, it makes no difference whether these changes are brought about by chemical injection or by a sense that our situation is dangerous. In fact, the aspiration here is precisely to give an absolute account of our emotions that makes no reference to the subjective experience of the agent. As we have seen, it may perhaps be possible to give such an account of physical fear, but we can now see what the upshot of such a theory will be, namely, an inability to distinguish fear from the sensations produced by chemical injection.

There is a second difficulty that arises for a noncognitive theory from its failure to account for the role of belief and judgment in our emotional lives. It is simply that a noncognitive theory cannot sanction an appeal to belief or judgment in the differentiation of particular emotional states. As we have seen, on James's view, emotions are distinguished one from another on the basis of introspection. Each emotion is thought to have both a distinct bodily state and a distinct feeling state associated with that bodily state. Indeed, perhaps the most direct legacy of James's work on the emotions was the search for these bodily states that followed in the wake of James's theory. Yet despite numerous attempts to identify distinct physiological states associated with particular emotions, little evidence for the existence of such states has been forthcoming. On the contrary, the evidence suggests that what is reported to be the same emotion can have different physical states associated with it and that the same physical states are associated with what are identified as very different emotions.[14] If distinct bodily states do not correspond to particular emotions, however, James can offer no account of how we differentiate particular emotional states.

Even apart from this lack of empirical evidence, however, we can appreciate the difficulties with James's approach to the differentiation of emotional states by reflecting on occasions where what or how one feels is uncertain. Recall our earlier discussion of the process of clarifying an emotion. We saw that if we have a vaguely negative emotional experience in response to viewing a film, we may clarify this emotional response by articulating our sense of the film. As we begin to articulate our sense of the film, our emotional response itself is made clear. On James's view, by contrast, uncertainty about one's feelings can only be the result of a sort of failure of attention: some distinct physical state—and with it a distinct feeling state—has been elicited by environmental cues, and one has simply failed to attend to these states. To get clear about how one feels, a person simply focuses attention on the preexisting feeling. Yet, as our earlier discussion indicates, the process of clarifying one's feelings is not like this at all.

Stuart Hampshire has made this point quite convincingly.[15] "Descriptions of states of mind, or beliefs, desires, and emotions," he writes, "are liable to a kind of indeterminacy which has no parallel in descriptions of physical states."[16] The upshot, he says, is that clarifying what one feels is very often more of a decision than a discovery; one makes up one's mind, one does not look for what is already there. Unfortunately, because a noncognitive theory of emotion reduces emotions to physical states, it necessarily misconstrues this process of clarification. Thus Hampshire provides an accurate assessment of James's mistake when he writes:

> recognizing what one thinks, feels, or wants, is apt to be wrongly assimilated to recognizing and identifying an independent physical object, where an independent object is something that can be observed by different observers from different points of view, and will change its appearance, but not its real properties, as the point of view changes. . . . But to become sure, by reflecting, what one's sentiments about or attitude to something, is one way, even the typical way, of forming or bringing into existence, that state of mind.[17]

James certainly does assimilate the recognition of emotions to the recognition of physical objects, and the upshot is that he cannot account for how emotions are individuated.

The Recovery of Self-Understanding II

If a noncognitive theory is thus deeply flawed, what is the alternative? The alternative here is a theory that does not regard emotions as biologically primitive sensations but sees them rather as complex experiences shaped in large part by culture. This is the theory that I wish to sketch in the remainder of this chapter. It is sometimes called a "cognitive" theory, sometimes a "constructivist" theory. By either name, it is a theory according to which an emotion is best understood, not, as with the traditional view, as a biologically basic and culturally invariant brute experience, but rather as a kind of cultural artifact. According to this view, emotions are culturally mediated or constructed experiences that are shaped by, and crucially dependent upon, cultural forms of discourse, such as symbols, beliefs, and judgments.

The contrast between a noncognitive view that regards emotions as biologically primitive and a constructivist one that sees emotions as cultural artifacts is roughly that between what the anthropologist Clifford Geertz has called a "stratigraphic" conception of human nature and a "synthetic" one. According to Geertz, a stratigraphic conception views psychological and sociocultural factors as just so many independent and distinct layers that can be stripped away until "one is left with the biological foundations—anatomical, physiological, neurological—of the whole edifice of human life."[18] We have seen that by focusing on the physiological responses characteristic of emotional experience James does indeed engage in a reductionistic attempt to strip away nonbiological components of human emotions. By contrast, a synthetic view of human nature, Geertz says, believes that psychological and sociocultural factors are ineludible. This is precisely what a constructivist theory says about psychological and sociocultural elements of human emotions.

The advantage of characterizing the contrast between cognitive and noncognitive theories in this way is that it allows us to see the fatal flaw, not only of James's account, but of all noncognitive accounts. It is the problem facing any stratigraphic conception of the relations between biological, psychological, and cultural factors in human life; it is this: the higher one gets on the evolutionary scale, the less narrowly is behavior determined by genetic structure. As Geertz makes clear, because what is innately given for humans are merely "extremely general response capacities," it follows that culture cannot be treated simply as an "ornament" of human existence that can be taken away without loss; rather, it must be treated as "the principal basis of its specificity" and as an "essential condition" for human life. Geertz puts the point vividly:

> Man without culture would not be the clever savages of Golding's *Lord of the Flies* thrown back upon the cruel wisdom of their animal instincts; nor would they be the nature's nobleman of Enlightenment primitivism or even, as classical anthropological theory would imply, intrinsically talented apes who had somehow failed to find themselves. They would be unworkable monstrosities, with very few useful instincts, fewer recognizable sentiments, and no intellect: mental basket cases.[19]

The claim that, without culture, humans would have few recognizable emotions is one that makes no sense on a noncognitive view. For on a noncognitive view emotions are biologically basic and thus essentially invariant from culture to culture, in part because they are precultural. By contrast, the claim that culturally unmediated emotions would be unrecognizable, or some similar claim, is at the heart of a constructivist view. On the constructivist view, emotions are complex experiences that cannot be reduced without remainder to biological foundations and are thus not culturally invariant. On this view, emotions may incorporate biologically basic and perhaps universal physiological components, but these components are molded into particular, recognizable emotional experiences through cultural mediation. The essence of a constructivist view is captured nicely by Geertz. "Even our emotions," he writes, "are, like our nervous system itself, cultural products—products manufactured, indeed, out of tendencies, capacities, and dispositions with which we were born, but manufactured nonetheless."[20]

Although the view that emotions are cultural achievements is a controversial one, it has gained an increasing number of supporters in recent years among both philosophers and psychologists.[21] Moreover, it has also received support from cultural anthropologists who, like Geertz, have attended to cross-cultural differences in emotional experience. One anthropologist who has forcefully pressed this point is Michelle Rosaldo. Rosaldo studied the Ilongot people of the Philippines and has written about the differences between Ilongot emotional experience and our own.[22] According to Rosaldo, although there is an emotion experienced by the Ilongot that can be translated into English as anger, the Ilongot experience of "anger" and our experience of anger are profoundly different. For us, anger is frequently understood to be a sort of psychic force which is dangerous to bottle up, lest pressure build to the point of explosion. Our language of anger is filled with what Robert Solomon calls "hydraulic" metaphors: we talk about "repressed" anger and about the need to "vent" our anger. According to Rosaldo, part of the reason we experience anger in this way is that our understanding of the self is one that allows for a sort of private interior space within which unexpressed psychic pressures can build up. The Ilongot people do no share this modern Western view of the self. For the Ilongot, the distinction between an interior, private sphere of personal emotions and a public realm in which private emotions can be expressed simply does not exist. Consequently, the Ilongot apparently do not experience anger as an explosive force. Indeed, the Ilongot appear to treat "anger" as a sort of public commodity.[23] For example, in Ilongot culture, it makes perfect sense to "pay" someone for his or her anger, at which point the anger is to be given up, handed over, so to speak, to the buyer. Rosaldo acknowledges that the Ilongot can be duplicitous about their emotions, but such duplicity is not a matter of hiding from public view an interior and private state. For example, it does not make sense, she says, for someone to receive pay for his anger and "then insist that a mere ritual is inadequate to resolve emotions that continue to be strong."[24] Rosaldo concludes from these differences that:

> affects, whatever their similarities, are no more similar than the societies in which we live: that ways of life and images of the self (the absence, in the Ilongot case, of an interior space in which the self might nurture an unconscious rage) decide what our emotions can be like in shaping stories of their likely cause and consequence. Ilongot discourse about "anger" overlaps with, yet is different from, our own. The same thing can be said about the things Ilongots feel. Or stated otherwise, the life of feelings is an aspect of the social world in which its terms are found.[25]

To say that emotions are culturally constructed, then, is to say with Rosaldo that, "feelings are not substances to be discovered in our blood but social practices organized by stories that we both enact and tell."[26] It is to say that emotions are crucially dependent on self-understanding and thus shaped by the social matrix within which self-understanding is formed and maintained. Indeed, the contrast between Ilongot culture and our own provides a striking illustration of the way in which self-understanding shapes our emotions and hence of the way in which emotions are embedded in social practices.

Emotion as Text

Rosaldo's claim that emotions are social practices organized by communal stories suggests that it might be worthwhile to return to the image invoked by James of emotion as text. As we saw, for James, this image conveyed what he took to be the primacy of religious experience in relation to philosophical or theological formulas concerning faith. For James the point of the metaphor was that in matters of faith one's private affective experiences are paramount. Yet, it seems to me that James's metaphor may be turned against him at this point. The image of emotion as text is indeed provocative, but not for the reason James supposed. The metaphor is instructive precisely because it points us away from a privatized account of emotional experience and toward a public one. Texts are always historically located. They emerge in particular times and particular places, and they reflect the contexts out of which they emerge. Insofar as texts are meaningful, they are so because they do more than simply report the private inner life of the individual author. They convey meaning in terms of publicly available and commonly shared symbols and experiences. In this sense, a private text, as Wittgenstein said of a private language, is simply not possible. Such a text is no text at all.

To say that emotions are texts, then, is to say more than that emotions stand to belief as a text to an interpreter. This is what James meant by saying that emotions are texts. Instead, to say that emotions are texts is to say that, like other texts, emotions tell a story. They are social practices that have a point. Because emotions are generated and sustained within communities of belief and practice, they tell us something about these communities. My anger tells a story. So does my pride. So does my joy. These emotions impart meaningful information, among other things, about what I, and the community of which I am a part, value most.

This is why I think Robert Solomon is right to speak about emotions as rule-governed interpretations of experience. Emotions are not just private, individualistic experiences. Rather, emotions are "part of an elaborate web of experience and belief" formed by community.[27] The idea of a web or network of belief in which every emotion has its place is tremendously fruitful. For one thing, such a conception allows us to make sense of our earlier claim that the evaluations, desires, and aspirations which constitute self-understanding are woven into our emotional lives. This account of emotion also allows us to appreciate how the sort of transformations we previously discussed are possible. If emotions are understood to involve a complex web of moral, scientific, and aesthetic beliefs, then a change in these beliefs has the potential for changing our emotions.

In fact, at this point Solomon offers a perspective on emotions that dovetails beautifully with my claim that we treat emotions as texts. Solomon talks about the need to develop a "hermeneutics of the passions." Such a project, he says, would investigate the dialectical relationship that I spoke of earlier between emotions and world views. This dialectic exists precisely because emotions have their place in a network of belief that includes what Solomon calls the "symbolic investments" which support our world view. Religious symbols, says Solomon, are good examples of the vital investments we make in our "chosen mythologies." The project for a hermeneutics of the passions, then, "is to uncover these symbolic investments, to see how they tie together and mutually support one another."[28] To put the point only slightly differently: a hermeneutics of the passions would seek to interpret the text of an emotion by investigating the cultural beliefs and values incorporated into particular emotional responses.

Solomon provides an extremely interesting example of this dialectic, one that highlights the relationship between emotions and self-understanding. Imagine a world view, he says, in which members of the group consider themselves to be "naturally superior" to other people. The upshot of this fundamental belief about oneself is that certain emotions "necessarily follow in particular circumstances." Here is Solomon's characterization of the process:

> One has invested in that self-image, and one cannot, except at great personal cost, give it up. So, as a form of protection (and not necessarily avoidance nor even "deception"), one becomes righteously indignant at casual insults, resentful of the smallest slight, prideful at the least chance. It may be extremely difficult to give up a self-image, and, consequently, to be able to give up any number of passions which support that image. But to say that it is "extremely difficult" is not to say that one cannot do so, nor is it to indicate in the slightest that those passions are caused and passive rather than intended and active.[29]

Solomon's specific point here is that we need to give up what he believes are the "degrading" emotions of pride and resentment, and that there is no hope of doing this until we begin to explore the conceptual connections between one's self-understanding as superior and the emotions of pride and resentment. But the more general point—and the one that is most relevant for us—is the importance of attending to the way in which symbolic investments both support, and are supported by, particular emotions. The reason this is relevant for us can be appreciated by imagining how very different the above situation would be if, instead of a self-image of "superiority," one viewed oneself as "corrupted by sin."

As this example helps to illustrate, the idea of emotion as text and of a hermeneutics of the passions reinforces our earlier sense of the importance of a cognitive theory of emotion to the study of religious ethics. Consider how, on a cognitive view, religious belief can transform one's emotional life. If emotions are constituted in part by basic judgments we make about the world, if they are, so to speak, scripted by communal beliefs and practices, then it follows that religious belief can play an absolutely crucial role in structuring our emotional lives for among the most notable beliefs and practices of many groups, beliefs and practices that can on this view give rise to and sustain particular emotions, will be those provided by religion.

We can also see here the connection between a cognitive or constructivist view of emotion and our previous discussion of the importance of self-understanding. The constructivist view that emotions are not simply biological givens, but rather are cultural achievements, helps us to make sense of the claim that self-understanding is crucial to human emotional life. As we have seen, a constructivist view is predicated on the notion that emotions are embedded in social practices circumscribed by language. In fact, to understand emotions as texts is to suggest that emotions are not only circumscribed by language, but are a sort of language by which we communicate with one another. If emotions are indeed a language by which we communicate with others, like other languages, they will be learned in community.

Emotions and Social Norms

Understanding emotions as a sort of language or text allows us to see that emotions are necessarily governed by social norms. This point is developed by the psychologist, James Averill, who attempts to give a determinate sense to the claim that emotions are embedded in social practices by introducing the notion of "feeling-rules."[30] According to Averill, because emotions essentially involve interpretations of our situations, it is possible to formulate various rules of interpretations governing emotional experience. There are two types of rules governing our emotional lives, constitutive rules and regulative rules. Constitutive rules are those rules that place a situation within a "hierarchy of meaning" such that we can count our response as, say, an episode of anger.[31] Regulative rules, by contrast, specify appropriate behavior once our situation is properly interpreted. Where constitutive rules specify what counts as anger, regulative rules specify what counts as appropriate angry behavior.

It is instructive to note here that Averill borrows this terminology from John Searle's work, *Speech Acts*.[32] This is instructive because Searle's discussion of the distinction between constitutive and regulative rules emerges against the backdrop of a general thesis about the rule-governed nature of language. Thus, by examining Searle's discussion and Averill's use of Searle's discussion, we may gain insight into the claim that emotions are a type of affective language. According to Searle, "speaking a language is engaging in a (highly complex) rule-governed form of behavior," and knowledge of how to speak a language "involves a mastery of a system of rules" that renders the use of elements of the language "regular and systematic."[33] Within this system of rules, says Searle, it is possible to distinguish rules that "create or define new forms of behavior," from rules that regulate "antecedently or independently existing forms of behavior."[34] The former Searle calls constitutive rules and the latter regulative. Further, according to Searle:

> Regulative rules characteristically have the form or can be comfortably paraphrased in the form "Do x" or "If y do x." Within systems of constitutive rules, some will have this form, but some will have the form "x counts as y," or "x counts as y in context c."[35]

It is important to note, says Searle, that in the case of constitutive rules, "the phrase which is the γ term will not in general simply be a label. It will mark something that has consequences."[36] In Searle's example, the constitutive rules of football, baseball, and chess are such that "touchdown," "home run," and "checkmate" are not mere labels for some state of affairs x, but rather have consequences in terms of scoring points, winning, and losing.

If we return to the thesis that there exist both constitutive and regulative feeling rules, I think we can appreciate how this point is simply an extension of the general nonstratigraphic conception of emotion that I have sought to articulate throughout this chapter. The point of talking about rules governing emotional behavior can be seen in connection with the observations made above about anger. Just as there is no state of affairs recognized as point scoring independent of a social practice in which one scores points by making a "touchdown," so there is no state of affairs recognized as anger independent of a social practice in which certain situations are understood to be ones in which "anger" is appropriate. Thus there is no point in trying to strip away the psychological and sociocultural factors here to reach the biological foundations; to attempt to do this would be like trying to score a touchdown without playing football: it cannot be done.

To say that our emotions are rule-governed and learned, however, is not to say that there exists explicitly articulated rules that are formally taught. The comparison of emotion to language suggests just the reverse: feeling rules would be like the rules of grammar. Like the rules of grammar, the rules governing emotional experience are not explicitly articulated but are internalized as individuals become members of a social group. Analogous to the role played by the rules of grammar, the rules governing our emotions structure emotional experience. They help to make emotional experience meaningful, and they make it possible to identify and censure departures from the emotional life of the community.

This last point is important because it highlights the two central features of the thesis that emotions are rule-governed: first, that it is possible to evaluate our emotions; and, second, that our emotions are socially established. As Peter Winch makes clear in his discussion of rule-following in *The Idea of a Social Science*, both of these features are characteristic of activity in conformity with rules. Discussing an example from Wittgenstein of an activity that is not rule-governed, Winch writes:

> Why is it not a rule? Because the notion of following a rule is logically insep-arable from the notion of making a mistake. If it is possible to say of someone that he is following a rule that means that one can ask whether he is doing what he does correctly or not. Otherwise there is no foothold in his behaviour in which the notion of a rule can take a grip; there is then no sense in describing his behaviour in that way, since everything he does is as good as anything else

he might do, whereas the point of the concept of a rule is that it should enable us to evaluate what is being done.

Winch goes on:

> Let us consider what is involved in making a mistake. . . . A mistake is a con-travention of what is established as correct; as such, it must be recognisable as such a contravention. That is, if I make a mistake in, say, my use of a word, other people must be able to point it out to me. If this is not so, I can do what I like and there is no external check on what I do; that is, nothing is estab-lished. Establishing a standard is not an activity which it makes sense to ascribe to any individual in complete isolation from other individuals. For it is con-tact with other individuals which alone makes possible the external check on one's actions which is inseparable from an established standard.[37]

Winch's comments here shed considerable light on the thesis that emotions are rule-governed experiences which draw our attention to the fact that it is possible to make a mistake in relation to our emotions, and that this is a possibility only if emotions, like language, are governed by social norms. To say, with Averill, that there are constitutive and regulative rules gov-erning emotions means that it is possible to evaluate both the application of emotion concepts and emotional behavior itself. The possibility of mak-ing evaluations here, the possibility of making mistakes in connection with our emotions clearly indicates that emotions are not just meaningless bio-logical forces but "meaning-full" experiences. As I said above, my anger tells a story. To announce that I am angry is not just to report some pri-vate inner state, rather it is to impart meaningful information, and this infor-mation will vary from culture to culture. In our group, it discloses that I stand in a certain relation to specific members of the community—an accusatory one; that I have particular beliefs and judgments that I expect would be endorsed by others—that I have been injured or harmed; that certain behavior is to be expected from me—hostility rather than friend-liness toward those who injured me. By contrast, to say that one is "angry" in Ilongot society imparts decidedly different information. The signifi-cance of saying that our emotions are rule-governed, then, is to point to the fact that anger can only be meaningful in this way if there are widely accepted social norms in a community that determine both when a person can be said to be angry and what can be expected from an angry person.

At this point, then, I think we can usefully supplement our previous dis-cussion of the features which distinguish a cognitive theory of emotions by noting how the two criteria previously introduced dovetail with the view that emotions are rule-governed. Recall that the distinguishing characteristics of the cognitive theory were that belief and judgment are constitutive fea-tures of the concept of emotion and necessary for individuating particular emotions. We can now see how these characteristics are joined to the rule-governed nature of emotions. We can see this by looking more closely at what Averill calls "rules of appraisal." According to Averill, a rule of appraisal is a constitutive rule that specifies the intentional object or objects of an emotion. Consider, once again, the example of pride. Pride must always be pride about something, and the rule of appraisal with respect to pride specifies what that something can be. In our culture, one violates a rule of appraisal with respect to pride if one claims to be proud of something one has not accomplished or which is not considered to be an honor. The point here is this: if pride were not rule-governed, if there was no rule governing the application of the concept of pride, then belief and judgment would not have a place among the defining characteristics of pride, nor would they be necessary for distinguishing pride from, say, joy. We can see, then, that it is because emotions are about something, and because there are social norms governing what particular emotions can be about, that belief and judgment can be said to have a place both among the defining characteristics of an emotion in general and among the features individuating particular emotions. Further, this means that self-understanding can shape emotions.

What, then, is an emotion? I suggest that we define an emotion as an experiential complex, shaped by social norms, that consists of such diverse elements as pronounced physiological activity, expressive bodily responses, feelings, desires, beliefs, and evaluative judgments.[38] Further, I suggest that we treat the cognitive components of the complex, beliefs and judgments, i.e., those components that embody self-understanding, as the keystone holding these various elements in place, for two reasons: (1) belief and judgment not only accompany the bodily responses characteristic of emotions, but cause them; and (2) without appeal to evaluative judgment we have no way of distinguishing emotional states, one from another.[39] On this account, then, cognitive judgment would lie at the heart of our emotional lives being connected to emotions both causally and conceptually. On the one hand, particular cognitive judgments are causally connected to a set of responses characteristic of particular emotions, and on the other hand, general evaluative categories are conceptually connected to particular emotion concepts.

With this definition in mind, we can return to Solomon's suggestive remarks about the significance of developing a hermeneutics of the passions as a way of concluding this chapter. We have seen that an evaluative judgment is a constitutive feature of an emotion, and the suggestion that our evaluations of the world are shaped in important ways by our cultural inheritance should now meet with little resistance. The upshot, of course, is that Solomon has rightly drawn our attention to something extremely important in highlighting the connection between emotions and symbolic investments. Further, I think it is the same connection Geertz meant to highlight by arguing that we are forced by our very natures to rely on extragenetic information for our ability to act at all. For, according to Geertz, once we realize that we must "rely more and more heavily on cultural sources—the accumulated fund of significant symbols," we will come to see that "such symbols are thus not mere expressions, instrumentalities, or correlates of our biological, psychological, and social existence; they are prerequisites of it."[40] It is similar with our emotions. Once we realize that without the structure provided by cultural rules governing our emotional lives, our emotions would be unrecognizable, chaotic, and alien, we come to see that reason is not opposed to emotion, nor, in a more Humean vein, a slave to it, and thus merely instrumental in relation to emotion. Rather, we come to see that reason is a constitutive feature of emotion.

This, at least, is what I hope this chapter has begun to suggest. We have seen that emotions are wrongly assimilated to sensations and feelings and that, when viewed as texts, emotions can be seen to have a sort of logic that cannot be violated with impunity. Violate the rules governing our emotional lives and emotions become, like the papers of those students who have not yet mastered the rules of grammar, meaningless and incoherent. What might be called emotional anomie sets in. As our earlier example suggested, we cannot, other things being equal, be proud of something we have not accomplished or of something we do not value. This is a point Wittgenstein highlighted in the *Investigations* when he wrote:

> "Grief," describes a pattern which recurs, with different variations, in the weave of our life. If a man's bodily expression of sorrow and of joy alternated, say with the ticking of a clock, here we should not have the characteristic formation of the pattern of sorrow or of the pattern of joy.[41]

To see what emotional anomie would amount to we need only imagine sorrow and joy alternating with a tick of the clock. To suggest that we could alternate between sorrow and joy from one second to the next would be to introduce a deep incoherence and fundamental irrationality into human life that a cognitive theory of the emotions is committed to rejecting.

Our emotional lives are not like that. Rather there is a coherence and constancy that frames our emotional lives, and this stability derives from the social practices in which our emotions are embedded. Emotions are indeed "meaning-full" structures, and they are structures, to use Wittgenstein's words, that are embedded in the weave of our life. This is why the idea of emotion as text is so suggestive: it captures the central insight of a cognitive theory, and it offers a perspective for accounting for how religious belief can transform one's emotions. There is constancy in our emotional lives because there are rules to which emotions, like any text, must conform if they are to be meaningful. Nevertheless, transformation of our emotional lives is possible precisely because the language that constitutes the text of our emotions may change. This is not, of course, to say that our emotions can simply be transformed at will by changing our beliefs or by adopting a new vocabulary. But it is to say that being part of a distinctive community, sharing in a distinctive moral or emotional vocabulary, or indeed entering into such a community, may result in the development of a distinctive emotional life. To see how this might be the case, let us consider, in the next two chapters, the social norms that appear to govern the experience of anger and resentment in the secular culture of the contemporary West and how this experience might be different in a different community of discourse.

4

The Emotions of
Anger and Resentment

We turn, at this point, to a consideration of the emotions of anger and resentment. I have already suggested that anger is not merely a biologically primitive feeling state that we label and report when we say that we are angry. On the contrary, I have claimed that anger, like most of our emotions, is socially constructed and thus governed by social norms.[1] What social norms govern the experience of anger in our culture? How are anger and resentment related? Are they governed by the same social norms? How do the social norms governing anger in our culture compare with those governing similar emotional experiences in other cultures? These are some of the questions we must try to answer in this chapter.

We can begin our discussion of anger, however, by acknowledging that the view that anger is socially constructed and governed by social norms is not the traditional view, and that we face the same obstacles in attempting to highlight the cognitive features of anger as we did in articulating the role of self-understanding in emotions generally. Anger has for so long been treated as opposed to reason and judgment, that it is hard to think of it in any other way. In this, Montaigne speaks for most of Western thought when he quotes Juvenal to support his view that no passion "so shakes the clarity of our judgment" as anger:

> Burning with rage within, they're borne
> Down headlong, just like boulders from a mountain torn;
> The ground gives way beneath, the hanging slope falls in.[2]

Anger is frequently portrayed in precisely this way, as a sort of natural force over which we have little control. Western literature is full of such examples. One thinks immediately of King Lear and his uncontrollable rage or of Medea and her self-destructive and violent anger. Our symbolic language of anger also supports this view. We speak, for example, of being "boiling mad," or "hot under the collar." The traditional view of anger, then, is clearly dominated by two motifs: on the one hand, that anger is uncontrollable, and, on the other, that it is violent and destructive.

To be sure, anger can be both uncontrollable and violent. Yet there is a danger in repeatedly highlighting these aspects of anger. To do so is to risk reducing anger to little more than a blind and destructive force. We know, however, that this is not a true picture of anger. Anger is often within our control, and its expression is often nonaggressive as well as nonviolent. Let us, therefore, try to sketch an account of anger that does not place undue emphasis on its blind and destructive side. We can begin this sketch by imagining an example of anger and noting some of its features. The case I have in mind is perhaps a trivial instance of anger, but it is one that most of us will recognize as real. Either we have experienced a similar anger or will likely know someone who has.

An Example of Anger

Imagine a homeowner named Kevin who takes great pride and pleasure in keeping his yard in shape. Kevin spends most weekend days during the summer tending his lawn. The bushes that hedge his property are full and well trimmed. The flower bed under the front bay window is colorful and weedless. There is a beautiful rose garden on the side of the house. The lawn itself is lush, green, and immaculate. Unfortunately (for Kevin), his neighbors have teenage sons, John and David, who neither care about beautiful yards in general nor about Kevin's yard in particular. John and David frequently play ball in their own yard, and, almost as frequently, their ball ends up in Kevin's yard; often, too, it ends up in Kevin's rose garden. Kevin is not happy about the situation and has repeatedly asked the boys not to cut through his hedge to retrieve their balls and indeed not to play where an errant throw leaves the ball in his yard. Kevin has also spoken to the boys' parents about the "problem."

Given this situation, it is not difficult to imagine that when the ball lands in Kevin's garden for the fifth time one afternoon, and the boys appear through the hedge to retrieve it, Kevin becomes genuinely angry. Indeed, some would describe what happens next as Kevin exploding. Kevin begins screaming at the two boys. He picks the ball up himself and refuses to return it. He threatens to call the police. When the boys, unrepentant and menacing, demand the ball back, Kevin throws the ball at them. Only the appearance of the boys' parents prevents the situation from escalating.

Admittedly, this is an insignificant example of anger, but certainly it is familiar. What does such an example reveal about anger? What features of anger are manifest in this case? First, we can note, with William James, that Kevin's anger is likely to include physiological changes and their attendant physical feelings. Kevin may well feel flushed; his heart may beat rapidly; he may be trembling. Moreover, Kevin will probably manifest what Averill calls expressive bodily reactions: his fists may be clenched, his eyes flashing. He may kick the bag of mulch in his anger. Indeed, at first blush, this episode seems to support the traditional view of anger. Kevin's anger is close to uncontrollable; his angry actions are violent. But note: although we might say that Kevin is overreacting,[3] that his anger is excessive, we would not say that his anger is irrational or unjustified. Yet, on the traditional view, because anger is thought of as a sort of storm that rolls in, as it were, it makes no sense to assess anger in this way. Yet we do. We say whether Kevin's anger is justified or not. We might argue, for example, that Kevin's anger is justified and that he has worked hard to get his lawn to look as nice as it does.[4] He has tried to be reasonable about the boys' ball-playing; he has asked them repeatedly to be more careful. Yet, evidently they do not care about Kevin's lawn. *And this is precisely why Kevin is angry.* He believes that he deserves more respect than he is being shown. He cares about his yard, and he has made it clear that he cares, and still the boys, who are old enough to know better, carelessly allow their balls to land in his rose bushes. In other words, Kevin's anger includes the belief that his interests are being harmed or, at the very least slighted, and that there is no good reason for this. In fact, we can see that without this belief Kevin's behavior would appear utterly mysterious. If, for example, Kevin clearly cared nothing at all about his lawn and indeed reported being both unconcerned about the ball just having landed in his yard and yet angry about this, we should say either that he does not know what "anger" is or that he is irrationally angry. Or suppose that the ball appears in Kevin's yard, but that it was not John or David who was responsible. Rather, it is their four-year-old brother. Kevin originally believes that John and David are responsible, and he is angry. When he discovers that they are not to blame, however, his anger leaves him. He realizes that he cannot expect such a young child to understand and respect his wishes.

This example of anger allows us to see, then, that in addition to the rather dramatic physical effects which can accompany anger, we must take into account the sense of a situation that appears to be a crucial component of anger, namely, that someone I care about has been harmed. And this belief helps us to see a second feature of anger: it will often include a desire that the harm in some way be redressed.[5] In our example, we might say that Kevin seeks to redress the harm by returning it in kind; he throws the ball at the boys to indicate his anger and lack of respect for them. Allowing a place for the belief that harm has been done and the desire that the perceived harm be redressed or prevented from happening again, however, begins to take us well beyond the traditional view of anger. For one thing, we can begin to see why anger can vary so greatly both in intensity and kind of expression, and why there can be such a great variety of occasions for anger. On the one hand, because anger rests on a sense that some harm has been done and because, under the appropriate conditions, almost any action (or inaction) could be construed as injurious or harmful, anger may arise in an infinite variety of situations. On the other hand, because the occasions of anger can be so various, so, too, will be the means of redressing a perceived harm. In some cases an angry desire to punish will be at work; in others a desire simply to elicit an apology; and in yet others a desire merely to see that the offender recognize that harm has been done so that it will not happen again.[6] In each of these cases, the desires may give rise to different forms of behavior. Physical aggression may be appropriate in one case, but radically inappropriate in another. Similarly, the intensity of one's anger can be seen to be determined, in part,[7] by the evaluation of the gravity or severity of the harm or injury. And there will be cases, like Kevin's, where the intensity of one's anger is excessive.

In fact, we can now see the precise sense of the claim, made in chapter 3, that cognition is the keystone holding together the various elements of emotional experience. Consider the elements of anger that we identified in our previous example. There is certainly a sense in which the various elements are related. The physiological activity (such as increased flow of adrenalin), for example, is clearly related both to the bodily expressions and psychic feelings that Kevin experiences as clenched fists and racing heart, and Kevin's behavior of throwing the ball is certainly related to his desire to punish. But what ties the package together, so to speak, is Kevin's judgment that some harm has been done. On the one hand, this judgment causes the physiological activity, on the other, it shapes both the desire to redress the injury and (thus) the behavior resulting from the injury. Indeed, the physiological activity, the feelings, and the bodily expressions are interpreted as constitutive of anger precisely because they are connected to the judgment that harm or injury has been done. Without this judgment, the experience would be opaque.

Moreover, we can also now appreciate the significance of the claim that emotions are best characterized as complex experiences which cannot be reduced to biological foundations. Characterizing emotions as complex states, which include psychological and sociocultural components, allows us to resist the temptation to set out necessary and sufficient conditions for emotions. We can see the wisdom of this position in connection to the emotion of anger, for it ought to be clear that we can be angry without clenching our fists or teeth, without striking out, without feeling flushed, even without having a desire to punish. The only feature which appears to be necessary to every instance of anger is the sense or concern that someone has been harmed. Nevertheless, these other elements are frequently aspects of the experience of anger, and they do appear to be connected. That they are allows us to say, with Wittgenstein, that there is a characteristic pattern to our emotions, and the important point is that the systematic character of the pattern is directly related to the cognitive judgments that I have argued characterize our emotions.

Self-Understanding and Anger—The Social Norms of Anger

If a sense of harm or injury is constitutive of the emotion of anger, are there also social norms governing anger, as we suggested in the previous chapter must be the case? I think that there are such norms, and we have already begun to sketch them. Again, however, it is important to be clear about what this claim involves as well as what it does not. I am not suggesting that there exist a set of rules which are explicitly articulated and consciously applied when the emotion of anger is experienced. Rather, I am suggesting that within our culture we find a number of norms that are widely accepted and that implicitly structure the experience of anger. It is the existence of such social norms with respect to anger, I believe, that makes it possible for us to evaluate and assess our anger, something we do quite often.

We saw in our previous example that it is possible to evaluate someone's anger. We might say of Kevin's anger that, while it is justified, it is nevertheless excessive. If we were to say this, it would make sense only if there are in fact social norms governing the experience of anger. We say of Kevin's anger that it is excessive precisely because there *is* a general consensus that anger should be roughly proportionate to its cause, and we want to say to Kevin that the damage to his rose bushes and his pride does not justify hurling a ball at his neighbors, that his response is disproportionate to their offense. It seems to me that we make such judgments all the time. Consider as further examples the following sorts of claims that we might well hear (and make) in reference to our own and other people's anger: (a) "You have no right to be angry with me, I didn't do anything"; (b) "Take it easy, it's not that big of a deal"; (c) "I could understand his action if it had been done out of anger, but that was done out of sheer spite"; (d) "He's not angry with you, he's just annoyed." We constantly make such assessments of anger; we judge it to be justified or unjustified, excessive or moderate, given up propitiously or unnecessarily protracted. That such judgments are appropriate is both a function of, and evidence for, the existence of social norms governing anger.

We saw in the last chapter that the social norms governing emotional experience can generally be sorted into two types: those governing the application of emotion concepts; and those regulating the emotional behavior itself. This is also true of the social norms of anger. There are norms about what properly counts as anger as well as norms about appropriate angry behavior. We have seen, for example, that one possible social norm governing angry behavior is that anger be roughly proportionate to the harm that has generated the anger. When this social norm is violated, we can expect social pressure for conformity to be exerted. When Kevin reacts violently to the ball landing in his yard, we expect others to point out to him that he is overreacting, for he has violated a social norm regarding angry behavior.[8] What of the norm(s) governing what counts as anger? We can perhaps identify such a norm by recalling our discussion of the various features typical of anger in our culture. We saw that the only feature that appeared to be a constituent of every instance of anger was the sense that harm had been done. Thus, if we were explicitly to formulate a rule governing the application of the concept of anger, it might be put as follows: anger is the appropriate description of an experience only where an individual believes she, or someone she cares about, has been harmed. But, of course, anger is more than the judgment that harm has been done. As we have seen, it can include increased physiological activity, expressive bodily reactions, overt behavior, and a variety of desires. Nevertheless, the concept of anger will not normally be applied to an experience in the absence of such responses, even if there exists a judgment that one has been harmed. So this norm is not a sufficient condition of the application of the concept of anger, but it does seem necessary. To say that I am angry in the absence of the belief that harm has been done, will be puzzling. If, for example, Kevin tells us that he does not feel harmed or slighted in any way by the boys' action, but that he is angry nonetheless, we would indeed be puzzled. As I suggested before, in all likelihood, we would believe that Kevin is either simply self-deceived or confused. Either he does in fact feel slighted in some way, although he is not consciously admitting it to himself or to us, or he is really angry at someone else, who has harmed him, and he is misdirecting his anger at the boys.

At this point it might be helpful to identify other social norms that appear to circumscribe the experience of anger in our culture. One apparent constraint placed on anger is that it be a response to a harm that is thought to be either intentional or easily avoidable. This is why anger is so frequently met by a denial that any harm was intended: lack of intentionality serves as a rebuttal to the accusation of anger. To the rule that anger is the appropriate description of an experience only where harm has been perceived, then, we might add one to this effect: angry behavior is appropriate only where a perceived harm is either thought to be intentional, or, where unintentional, is thought to be something that easily could have been, and should have been avoided. This is why, for example, if John and David's younger brother threw the ball into Kevin's yard, and Kevin knows this, his anger would be inappropriate.

The fact that angry behavior seems constrained by such a norm itself suggests that an attribution of responsibility is a background condition of anger. Thus we might expect that in our culture anger will be considered appropriate only toward responsible agents. What other norms governing anger might we expect? Because anger seems fundamentally to involve a desire to respond to a perceived harm, we might expect that angry action will be sanctioned only to the extent that it is directed to redressing that harm. Part of the reason that Kevin's angry actions will meet with disapprobation is that they are so counterproductive. By throwing the ball at the boys he does not properly redress the situation; he makes it worse. And, finally, insofar as anger is directed to redressing a perceived offense, we might expect a norm to the effect that anger should end when redress has been made. If Kevin remains angry even after the boys have apologized and have made efforts to see that it does not happen again, we would probably say that his continued anger is unjustified. We might, for example, accuse Kevin of vindictiveness. We would expect him to give up his grudge.

Now although none of these norms is explicitly articulated, social pressure to conform to these norms does seem to exist. There is a perceived inappropriateness about anger at inanimate objects[9] or at unintentional acts; or about anger directed at the wrong person, or anger that lingers long after the wrong has been righted. We do not expect anger to take these forms and when it does, it will not likely be socially accepted. I do not mean to suggest by this that the anger of everyone in our culture always conforms to these norms. Obviously, this is not the case. We can be angry at the unintentional slight or at the damned night table on which we have just stubbed our toe, but these are not the norm. The point here is that there are social norms, which govern the experience of anger in our culture, that are shared widely enough to create a pattern of activity which has social meaning. Here, then, we can begin to see the plausibility of the central thesis of chapter 3: that emotions are, in large measure, cultural products for both the standards themselves, and the specification of these standards, are the products of social life. If anger is to be the emotional response of individuals in a community to the perception of intentional harm or injury, and if anger is to be directed to redressing this harm and is to be roughly proportionate to the degree of harm, then the experience of anger will be thoroughly saturated with, and shaped by, the social norms of the community of which we are a part. What counts as harm, as adequate redress, as intentional injury, etc., will be determined by social norms. This is why Solomon's claim that, "to understand another person's emotional life requires nothing less than an understanding of their view(s) of the world as a whole" is plausible.[10] As we have just seen, Solomon is right when he says that an emotion is not an isolated judgment but rather is a "part of an elaborate web of experience and belief, tied to other judgments." In our example, anger is tied to judgments about injury, harm, agency, adequate reparation, and so on.

We can see that in addition to specifying both the minimal conditions for the application of emotion concepts and the rules of appropriateness structuring particular emotions, cultural norms shape emotional experience in a third way for it seems true that even general cultural lore about emotions molds, almost imperceptively, emotional experience. Indeed, we have already seen one illustration of this point in the contrast between the experience of anger in our culture and that in Ilongot culture. Our experience of anger is indeed shaped by the "hydraulic" model of emotional experience. Traceable in its current version primarily to Freud,[11] the view that emotions are psychic forces or energies pulsing through our bodies, demanding release, has clearly affected both our thinking about, and our experience of, the emotion of anger. Consider, for example, the popular wisdom that anger ought to be expressed, that it should not be "bottled up," that to fail to allow its release is to court disaster in the form of a more massive explosion of accumulated forces. Rosaldo is undoubtedly correct that this understanding of anger is not possible where the self is conceptualized in a way that fails to provide an interior space in which these pressures can build up. But neither could this understanding of anger be maintained in a cultural space that did not employ hydraulic metaphors for thinking about emotions.

"Anger" in Other Cultures

We are not likely to be able to appreciate this point at first because we have no distance on our own emotional experiences. We tend to experience anger as an explosive eruption of built-up psychic forces because it is this hydraulic vocabulary which frames our culture's experience of anger. But, as Rosaldo's work demonstrates, we could experience our anger differently, and, if we did, it would perhaps make more sense to say we experienced a different emotion than to say that we experienced the same emotion differently. To try to get clear about this claim, let us look briefly at a second example of the experience of "anger" in another culture,[12] one taken from Grace Gredys Harris's study of the Taita people of Kenya, *Casting Out Anger.*[13] As the title of the book suggests, this work is a study of the Taita view of anger, and it provides a richly detailed account of the Taita ritual for casting out anger, the central religious ritual of this group. The Taita cast out anger, not because they fear—as we might—the buildup of repressed psychic energies, but because they view anger as a dangerous mystical force. For the Taita, anger directed at certain persons under certain circumstances can lead to the misfortune of the target. Personal illness, death of livestock, indeed, just about any mishap can be the result of incurring someone's anger. As a result, Professor Harris tells us:

Being divined-for in terms of angry hearts was an experience shared by all adult *Batasi*[14] whatever their stage of the life cycle, whatever their sex, age, lineage membership, wealth or political advancement. Divination for anyone might identify misfortune as the result of incurring the anger of a living person or one of the dead.[15]

This identification of the source of one's misfortune in another's anger is in turn the prelude to the ritual act of *kutasa*, casting out anger. Harris describes *kutasa* this way:

Spraying out mouthfuls of liquid, the performer uttered phrases, exhorting or supplicating a mystical agent or agents and calling down blessings on one or more living humans and on what pertained to their welfare. At some point the utterances explicitly or implicitly rejected the angry feelings of the performer himself. As an act believed efficacious, *kutasa* was asserted to have an inner aspect of which spraying-and-speaking was the outward and audible form. The state of the performer's "heart" (*ngolo*) was intrinsic to the performance, since only from a heart "clean" and "cool," freed from anger and resentment, could the necessary sincere utterances issue. *Kutasa* in itself provided the means both to effect the final casting out of anger and resentment from the performer's heart and to turn away the anger of the agent(s) addressed.[16]

Apart from the fascination of the ritual itself, the most interesting thing about Harris's discussion of the Taita *kutasa* is the elaborate set of rules which, she suggests, governs the recognition, acknowledgment, and resolution of anger in this culture. Among the rules Harris mentions are the following: (a) under normal conditions, strangers cannot be the source of mystically dangerous anger; (b) a serious illness of someone other than a child should be attributed to the anger of a close consanguineous kinsman; (c) a husband's anger at his wife can be dangerous to him; (d) a child's anger at a parent can be dangerous to the child; (e) refusal to perform *kutasa* after divination had shown one's heart to be angry is considered sorcery; and (f) for certain offenses placation gifts (*kuvoya*) are required.

Although the rules Harris explicitly mentions do not directly correspond to our own social norms regarding anger, nevertheless, there is room for comparison. Specifically, the Taita appear to share our view that anger is the appropriate response to perceived harm, for, according to Harris, the mystical anger of humans is aroused "by ignoring or transgressing their rights, or simply by callous, inconsiderate behaviour."[17] Moreover, although the Taita direct their anger at things besides human beings, they seem to share our view that anger is only appropriately aroused where agency is active. Further, the Taita also appear to share the norm that anger should be proportional to the severity of the offense. They differ most dramatically from us, however, in their conception of the actions appropriate to anger and in their view of when anger should end. Recall that I suggested that our view on these two points could be set out in terms of social norms to the effect that anger should be directed toward redressing an offense and that anger should cease when the offense has been redressed. With the Taita, however, things are very different. Because the Taita believe that the anger itself can be causally efficacious in redressing a wrong, there is little reason to proscribe certain retaliatory behavior as inappropriate for the angered party; the anger takes care of itself, so to speak.[18] In fact, because the mystical powers of anger are so uncontrollable and so dangerous—they threaten not only the offender but others as well— the primary responsibility for resolving a dispute falls, not on the original offender, but on the injured party. Indeed, in what can only appear paradoxical from our point of view, for any given occasion of anger, the greatest measure of culpability is likely to fall to the injured party. The supposed danger of the mystical anger is also the reason why, for the Taita, anger must cease regardless of whether the offender has made amends. Thus, according to Harris, as long as she was there, no one ever refused to do *kutasa* when named by divination as the source of mystical misfortune (81). In fact, it is common for a Taita to recall being offended by someone suffering severe illness in order to do *kutasa* and thus dispel their "anger" toward the sick "offender."

This comparison of two different cultures' experience of anger highlights once again just how accurate Solomon is in his claim about the need to understand a group's view of the world as a whole in order to understand the emotional life of the group. I think this is evident in the case of the Taita, and if the passages I have cited thus far have not made this clear, the following one should:

> For Taita, the hot/cool contrast was not only metaphorical, but constitutive of reality. This "constitutive metaphor" is a common one which Taita put to use in their own special way in the context of a hill homeland surrounded by black plains. The heat of the dry, game-ridden bush was equated with anger, and the coolness of the high peaks with absence of anger in a heart that was clean and at peace. Topocosm and psychocosm were structured in the same way, with the polarities of hills/plains and peaceful heart/angry heart running through the ritual system. Other polarities were congruent: inside outside; social antisocial; Taita non-Taita. What was bad to have inside the person, namely anger, had to be cast outside; its affinity was with the heat of the plains, with the antisocial acts of thieving, perjury and violence, and with dangerous alien influences. The good inside of the person whose heart had been purged of anger was linked to the coolness of the peaks, with proper behaviour and with being truly Taita. Communities had to purge themselves of sorcerers, the embodiment of heat, anger, violence and treachery, and to be filled with peaceful, right-acting and loyal citizens.[19]

The Taita experience of anger, then, is intimately connected to an entire world view. Can there be any doubt that what they experience when they report being "angry" and what this means is radically different from what we experience and what we mean when we report that we are angry? For the Taita, the experience of anger is mystically dangerous and thus the trajectories of angry behavior are very different in Taita culture from those in our own. The social articulation of our emotional lives is here very much in evidence. As we return to our own culture, I hope it is clear that the complexity of the norms governing anger, and their connection to more comprehensive understanding of the world, is not limited to traditional cultures like the Taita, but is characteristic also of our own.

A Literary Test Case—*The Grapes of Wrath*

I have suggested that there are social norms which govern the experience of anger in our culture, and I have tried to sketch a number of such norms. But are these claims plausible? Is the emotion of anger really embedded in a web of experience and belief within our culture? To answer these questions, I invite the reader to consider these questions in light both of his or her own experiences, but also in light of examples taken from literature. Let me try to lend plausibility to my claims, then, by considering examples of anger from a classic work in American fiction, John Steinbeck's *The Grapes of Wrath*.[20] Whatever the other literary merits or faults of this work—and critics are divided over this point[21]—few, I think, would question its status as a superb study of the experience of anger.

The book tells the story of a family of Oklahoma farmers, the Joads, who are forced, as a result of a series of crop failures, to first become sharecroppers on the land they once owned, then to leave the land that had been the Joad home for generations, and, finally, to become migrant farmers as they move to California in search of work. Set in the Depression of the 1930s, it is a story of the bigotry and mistreatment the Joads endure as they work for slave wages in the fields of California. It is a story of the humiliation of being treated as a "goddamn Okie,"[22] as less than fully human, and of the anger that such mistreatment generates. Indeed, much of the dramatic action of the book revolves around the Joads' response to this mistreatment, as Steinbeck brilliantly portrays his characters' reactions—anger prominent among them. Yet, what is compelling both about the work in general and about Steinbeck's treatment of anger in particular is the realistic quality of the emotional lives of the characters. The emotional reactions of the characters are not emotional cliches; there is a richness and diversity here that reflects real life. In the case of anger, Steinbeck does not merely portray the stereotypical instance of explosive and physically violent rage—though there is that—but also an extraordinarily poignant and highly symbolic expression of anger. Let us turn, then, to several examples of angry episodes from *The Grapes of Wrath* and see whether the norms we have sketched above are in evidence. Although I will indicate, very briefly, which of the norms I think is applicable to each of the incidents when it is presented, I will reserve extended comment until all four examples are before us.

Example 1

The first incident takes place toward the beginning of the Joad family's flight from Oklahoma when they stop to get gas and encounter for the first time the mistrust and suspicion that being homeless and on the road elicits. Instead of the friendly greeting to which they were accustomed in their hometown, they are met by the "truculent and stern" proprietor's accusation:

> "You folks aim to buy anything? Gasoline or stuff?" he asked.
> Al [Joad] was out already, unscrewing the steaming radiator cap with the tips of his fingers, jerking his hand away to escape the spurt when the cap should come lose. "Need some gas, mister."
> "Got any money?"
> "Sure. Think we're beggin'?"
> The truculence left the fat man's face. "Well, that's all right, folks. He'p yourself to water." And he hastened to explain. "Road is full a people, come in, use water, dirty up the toilet, an' then, by God, they'll steal stuff an' don't buy nothin'. Got no money to buy with. Come beggin' a gallon a gas to move on."
> Tom [Joad] dropped angrily to the ground and moved toward the fat man. "We're payin' our way," he said fiercely. "You got no call to give us a goin'-over. We ain't asked you for nothin'."
> "I ain't," the fat man said quickly. The sweat began to soak through his short-sleeved polo shirt. "Jus' he'p yourself to water, and go use the toilet if you want." (GW, 170–71)

This episode is interesting because, as it unfolds, it becomes clear that the proprietor's truculence is not really directed at the Joads; that it is not intended to do harm; that it is, rather, a shield against the acceptance of his own poverty. By the end of the episode, Steinbeck has made it clear that Tom's anger is inappropriate, and we can see why: there is general consensus in our culture that anger is really only appropriate where intentional harm has been done and it should be proportional to that harm.

> The fat man pumped the gasoline and the needle turned on the pump dial, recording the amount. "Yeah, but what's it [the country] comin' to? That's what I want ta know."
> Tom broke in irritably, "Well, you ain't never gonna know. Casy tries to tell ya an' you jest ast the same thing over. I seen fellas like you before. You

ain't askin' nothin'; you're jus' singin' a kinda song. 'What we comin' to?' You don' wanta know. Country's movin' aroun', goin' places. They's folks dyin' all aroun'. Maybe you'll die pretty soon, but you won't know nothin'. I seen too many fellas like you. You don't want to know nothin'. Just sing yourself to sleep with a song—'What we comin' to?'" He looked at the gas pump, rusted and old, and at the shack behind it, built of old lumber, the nail holes of its first use still showing through the paint that had been brave, the brave yellow paint that had tried to imitate the big company stations in town. But the paint couldn't cover the old nail holes and the old cracks in the lumber, and the paint could not be renewed. The imitation was a failure and the owner had known it was a failure. And inside the open door of the shack Tom saw the oil barrels, only two of them, and the candy counter with stale candies and licorice whips turning brown with age, and cigarettes. He saw the broken chair and the fly screen with a rusted hole in it. And the littered yard that should have been graveled, and behind, the corn field drying and dying in the sun. Beside the house the little stock of used tires and retreaded tires. *And he saw for the first time the fat man's cheap washed pants and his cheap polo shirt and his paper hat.* He said, "I didn't mean to sound off at ya, mister. It's the heat. You ain't got nothin'. Pretty soon you'll be on the road yourse'f. And it ain't tractors'll put you there. It's them pretty yella stations in town. Folks is movin'," he said ashamedly. "An' you'll be movin', mister." (GW, 173–74)

Example 2

The second incident I want to record needs almost no introduction. It occurs after the Joads have been forced, under threat of being burned out, to flee a migrant camp for no reason other than that "goddamn red troublemakers" are not welcome. In contrast to the first example, Steinbeck leaves no doubt that Tom's anger is righteous anger; in our terms, it is socially accepted anger because Tom is indeed being mistreated.

"Come on, Pa. Let's go. Look here, Pa. You an' me an' Al ride in the seat. Ma can get on the load. No. Ma, you ride in the middle. Al"—Tom reached under the seat and brought out a big monkey wrench—"Al, you get up behind. Take this here. Jus' in case. If anybody tries to climb up—let 'im have it."

Al took the wrench and climbed up the back board, and he settled himself cross-legged, the wrench in his hand. Tom pulled the iron jack handle from under the seat and laid it on the floor, under the brake pedal. "Awright," he said. "Get in the middle, Ma."

Pa said, "I ain't got nothin' in my han'."

"You can reach over an' get the jack handle," said Tom. "I hope to Jesus you don' need it." He stepped on the starter and the clanking flywheel turned over, the engine caught and died, and caught again. Tom turned on the lights and moved out of the camp in low gear. The dim light fingered the road nervously. They climbed up to the highway and turned south. Tom said, "They comes a time when a man gets mad."

Ma broke in, "Tom—you tol' me—you promised me you wasn't like that. You promised."

"I know, Ma. I'm a-tryin'. But them deputies—Did you ever see a deputy that didn't have a fat ass? An' they waggle their ass an' flop their gun aroun'. Ma," he said, *"if it was the law they was workin' with, why, we could take it. But it ain't the law. They're a-workin' away at our spirits.* They're a-tryin' to make us cringe an' crawl like a whipped bitch. They tryin' to break us. Why, Jesus Christ, Ma, they comes a time when the on'y way a fella can keep his decency is by takin' a sock at a cop. They're workin' on our decency. . . .

The car jolted along. Ahead, a little row of red lanterns stretched across the highway.

"Detour, I guess," Tom said. He slowed the car and stopped it, and immediately a crowd of men swarmed about the truck. They were armed with pick handles and shotguns. They wore trench helmets and some American Legion caps. One man leaned in the window, and the warm smell of whisky preceded him.

"Where you think you're goin'?" He thrust a red face near to Tom's face.

Tom stiffened. His hand crept down to the floor and felt for the jack handle. Ma caught his arm and held it powerfully. Tom said, "Well-" and then his voice took on a servile whine. "We're strangers here," he said. "We heard about they's work in a place called Tulare."

"Well, goddamn it, you're goin' the wrong way. We ain't gonna have no goddamn Okies in this town."

Tom's shoulders and arms were rigid, and a shiver went through him. Ma clung to his arm. The front of the truck was surrounded by the armed men. Some of them, to make a military appearance, wore tunics and Sam Browne belts.

Tom whined, "Which way is it at, mister?"

"You turn right around an' head north. An' don't come back till the cotton's ready."

Tom shivered all over. "Yes, sir," he said. He put the car in reverse, backed around and turned. He headed back the way he had come. Ma released his arm and patted him softly. And Tom tried to restrain his hard smothered sobbing.

"Don' you mind," Ma said. "Don' you mind."

Tom blew his nose out the window and wiped his eyes on his sleeve. "The sons-of-bitches—"

"You done good," Ma said tenderly. "You done jus' good." (GW, 380–82; my emphasis)

Tom makes it clear that the treatment the Joads are receiving is unjustified. They are breaking no laws, and they are doing nothing wrong. Yet they are being mistreated. Their anger is a righteous anger with which we can empathize.

Example 3

The third example is that of Tom's violent and uncontrollable anger at the murder of his good friend, Jim Casy. The episode falls into three stages: (i) Tom's own murderous anger; (ii) his revelation of the incident to the family; and (iii) his mother's attempt to understand it. The example illustrates that even violent and apparently uncontrollable anger may be socially acceptable under certain conditions. The episode begins with Tom and Casy being chased by men looking to break a strike organized by Casy.

i

"Le's go," said Casy.

They moved quietly along the edge of the stream. The black span was a cave before them. Casy bent over and moved through. Tom behind. Their feet slipped into the water. Thirty feet they moved, and their breathing echoed from the curved ceiling. Then they came out on the other side and straightened up.

A sharp call, "There they are!" Two flashlight beams fell on the men, caught them, blinded them. "Stand where you are." The voices came out of the darkness. "That's him. That shiny bastard. That's him."

Casy stared blindly at the light. He breathed heavily. "Listen," he said, "you fellas don' know what you're doin'. You're helpin' to starve kids."

"Shut up, you red son-of-a-bitch."

A short heavy man stepped into the light. He carried a new white pick handle. Casy went on, "You don' know what you're a-doin'."

The heavy man swung with the pick handle. Casy dodged down into the swing. The heavy club crashed into the side of his head with a dull crunch of bone, and Casy fell sideways out of the light.

"Jesus, George. I think you killed him."

"Put the light on him," said George. "Serve the son-of-a-bitch right." The flashlight beam dropped, searched and found Casy's crushed head.

Tom looked down at the preacher. The light crossed the heavy man's legs and the white new pick handle. Tom leaped silently. He wrenched the club free. The first time he knew he had missed and struck a shoulder, but the second time his crushing blow found the head, and as the heavy man sank down, three more blows found his head. The lights danced about. There were shouts, the sound of running feet, crashing through brush. Tom stood over the prostrate man. And then a club reached his head, a glancing blow. He felt the stroke like an electric shock. And then he was running along the stream, bending low. (GW, 526–27)

ii

"What the hell is this?" Pa demanded [of Tom].

"I'm a-gonna tell. Las' night I went out to see what all the yellin' was about. An' I come on Casy."

"The preacher?"

"Yeah, Pa. The preacher, on'y he was a-leadin' the strike. They come for him."

Pa demanded, "Who come for him?" "I dunno. Same kinda guys that turned us back on the road that night. Had pick handles." He paused. "They killed 'im. Busted his head. I was standin' there. I went nuts. Grabbed the pick handle." He looked bleakly back at the night, the darkness, the flashlights, as he spoke. "I-I clubbed a guy."

Ma's breath caught in her throat. Pa stiffened. "Kill 'im?" he asked softly.

"I-don't know. I was nuts. Tried to. . . ."

"Yeah! Pa. You see? Casy was still a—good man. Goddamn it, I can't get that pitcher outa my head. Him layin' there—head jus' crushed flat an' oozin'. Jesus!" He covered his eyes with his hand. (GW, 532–33)

iii

She [Ma] sat down on the edge of his mattress. "You got to tell me," she said. "I got to figger how it was. I got to keep straight. What was Casy a-doin'? Why'd they kill 'im?"

"He was jus' standin' there with the lights on' 'im."

"What'd he say? Can ya 'member what he says?"

Tom said, "Sure. Casy said, 'You got no right to starve people.' An' then this heavy fella called him a red son-of-a-bitch. An' Casy says, 'You don' know what you're a-doin'.' An' then this guy smashed 'im."

Ma looked down. She twisted her hands together. "Tha's what he said— 'You don' know what you're doin?'"

"Yeah!"

Ma said, "I wisht Granma could a heard."

"Ma—I didn' know what I was a-doin', no more'n when you take a breath. I didn' even know I was gonna do it."

"It's awright. I wisht you didn' do it. I wisht you wasn' there. But you done what you had to do. I can't read no fault on you." (GW, 535)

Once again I think Steinbeck presents us with an example of righteous anger. In this case, Tom's friend Casy is murdered for no reason, and Tom responds with violent anger. Yet his anger is not unprovoked, as Ma fully realizes. She wants to understand what happened, and when she does, she renders her verdict: "I can't read no fault on you," she says.

Example 4

The last example is, I think, an exceptionally moving and poignant illustration of anger. The incident occurs toward the end of the book after the Joads have suffered and endured poverty for months. During this entire period Tom's sister, Rose of Sharon, has been pregnant and has worried about the effects of their horrid living conditions on the baby. When she finally delivers her baby in an old railroad boxcar that is then the Joads' home, her worst fears are realized: the child is stillborn. At this point, Uncle John is asked to take the dead child out into the heavy rains which are flooding the area and to bury the child.

> Pa turned to Uncle John. "Will you take an' bury it while Al an me git that lumber in?"
> Uncle John said sullenly, "Why do I got to do it? Why don't you fellas? I don' like it." And then, "Sure. I'll do it. Sure, I will. Come on, give it to me." His voice began to rise. "Come on! Give it to me."
> "Don't wake 'em [Rose of Sharon and Ma Joad] up," Mrs. Wainwright said. She brought the apple box to the doorway and straightened the sack decently over it.
> "Shovel's standin' right behin' you," Pa said.
> Uncle John took the shovel in one hand. He slipped out the doorway into the slowly moving water, and it rose nearly to his waist before he struck bottom. He turned and settled the apple box under his other arm.
> Pa said, "Come on, Al. Le's git that lumber in."
> In the gray dawn light Uncle John waded around the end of the car, past the Joad truck; and he climbed the slippery bank to the highway. He walked down the highway, past the boxcar flat, until he came to a place where the boiling stream ran close to the road, where the willows grew along the road side. He put his shovel down, and holding the box in front of him, he edged through the brush until he came to the edge of the swift stream. For a time he stood watching it swirl by, leaving its yellow foam among the willow stems. He held the apple box against his chest. And then he leaned over and set the box in the stream and steadied it with his hand. He said fiercely, "Go down an' tell 'em. Go down in the street an' rot an' tell 'em that way. That's the way you can talk. Don' even know if you was a boy or a girl. Ain't gonna find out. Go on down now, an' lay in the street. Maybe they'll know then." He guided the box gently out into the current and let it go. It settled low in the water, edged sideways, whirled around, and turned slowly over. The sack floated away, and the box, caught in the swift water, floated quickly away, out of sight, behind the brush. (GW, 608–9)

The significance of these four examples is found in the fact that they are at once convincing and illustrative of almost all of the points I have urged in my account of anger. We see in these examples that anger can be expressed (examples 1, 3, and 4) or inhibited (example 2); that it can take a verbally aggressive form (1) or a physically aggressive form (2 and 3) or nonaggressive form (4); it can include expressive bodily reactions (1, 2, and probably 3) or not (4); it can be controllable (1, 2, 4) or uncontrollable (3); it can include strong physiological manifestations (1, 2, 3) or not (4).

Moreover, these examples help us to appreciate the central role of evaluation and appraisal and hence of the social norms governing anger. In each case, the anger is generated by the belief that some harm has been done intentionally, and, as the first example indicates, when this judgment is not present, or when it fades, anger does not seem to be the appropriate response. Steinbeck has Tom apologetic and ashamed at the end of the first incident, and rightly so. The attendant meant no harm, and any offense he might have given was due more to fear than anything else. As Tom realizes by the end of the episode, the target of his anger may well be worse off than the Joads, and this realization moves Tom to abandon his anger. Other norms are exhibited in these examples as well. In the second incident we see highlighted the significance of the judgment that an offense is unjustifiable as well as intentional. Tom tells us that if the laws were being followed, if moving the migrants from the camp was justified, he could take it. But, as he puts it, it "ain't the law," and this is why he is angry. Further, we here see Ma imploring Tom to control his anger to keep it proportionate, not to act on it when it would clearly do no good. Just in these first two examples, then, we see exhibited many of the social norms previously identified. Anger is acceptable only where intentional harm has been done; anger should be proportionate; and it should be constructively directed toward correcting the offense.

Yet, despite the usefulness of these first two examples, I think it is examples (3) and (4), and, in particular, the contrast between them, that reveals in full measure the complexity of the experience of anger, both in Steinbeck and in our own lives. Example 3, of course, is an almost perfect instantiation of the traditional paradigm of anger: Tom is out of control and violent; in Juvenal's words, he is "borne down headlong, like a boulder from a mountain torn." Example 4, on the other hand, could not be further from the traditional view. Uncle John is in complete control; his anger is self-conscious; and it is neither violent nor particularly aggressive. Should we say that his anger is any less real or less palpable for that? The answer, it seems clear to me, is that we should not. I suggest that these two examples be treated as opposing ends of the continuum, one end of which is rooted in biology, the other end of which is rooted in culture.[23] That this is a useful way of approaching these examples can be appreciated by noting how similar Tom's angry action is to the biologically basic instinct of striking out at a source of pain. Alternatively, consider how far removed Uncle John's response is to anything biologically instinctive or determined. In saying that Tom's action is illustrative of that end of the emotional spectrum which is biologically anchored, however, I am not suggesting that Tom's experience is irrational or meaningless. We have seen, on the contrary, that, despite Tom's claims he was not in control, that he "went nuts." Ma still calls Tom to account for his anger and still makes an assessment, deeming his anger appropriate. Part of the power of this scene comes from the empathetic emotional response of the reader. Tom is not treated properly; nor is Casy, and as readers we respond with anger as did Tom.

These two examples also help to illustrate my earlier claim that anger is a "meaning-full" experience, and that to express one's anger is not merely to make public some private inner state, but to engage in a social practice that is governed by norms. These points are easier to see in connection with Uncle John's anger, because his anger is such a clear and poignant statement of accusation, and this is indeed the meaning of anger. *The expression of anger is an accusation of wrongdoing.* "'Go down an' tell 'em. Go down in the street an' rot an' tell 'em that way,'" Uncle John says. He means: "Tell those that have paid slave wages, that have treated the migrant workers worse than animals, that they are responsible for the death of the baby, that they stand accused. Tell them that we demand an explanation and that restitution is due." Yet, for all the power of Uncle John's expression of anger, it is no more accusatory than is Tom's action. True, Tom accuses, convicts, and punishes all in an instant, but the accusation of anger is there nonetheless, as Ma properly realizes. This is why she asks for an explanation of Tom's anger, of his accusation. "'You got to tell me,'" she says, "'I got to figger how it was. I got to keep straight. What was Casy a-doin'? Why'd they kill 'im.'" What she wants to know here is whether Tom's charge is justified. If Casy provoked the attack on him, then Tom's anger might well have been unjustified, and hence his actions wrong. Because the attack on Casy was unprovoked, however, she concludes that Tom was justified. "'I can't read no fault on you,'" she says.

Taken together, then, these four examples help us to see that anger is indeed a socially constructed emotional experience, that the expression of anger has meaning in a social setting, that anger is composed of many elements held together by the judgment that harm or injury has been done, and that this judgment connects anger to a web of experience and belief that both helps create, and is part of, a general world view.

Further, these examples also help us to see that anger and resentment are not two completely distinct emotional responses. Rather resentment is a form of anger, what might be called moral anger.[24] We can see this in our examples of anger from the *Grapes of Wrath*, because while each of these episodes is clearly an example of anger, certainly the third and fourth episodes are also instances of resentment. When Tom tells Ma that there comes a point where a person just gets mad, he makes it clear that he resents being treated, as he puts it, as a "whipped bitch." He is tired of being treated as less than fully human. He wants respect. He is morally indignant at the treatment he is receiving, and his response is one of anger. But it is anger of a certain sort. It is anger at a harm or injury that is morally wrong.

Resentment as Moral Anger

To explicate the claim that resentment is best understood as moral anger, it may be useful to turn briefly to Bishop Butler's discussion of resentment, for his account of resentment is remarkably close to the one I am suggesting here. Butler's position is simply the converse of my own: for him anger is not the genus, but the species; anger, he says, is a form of resentment. According to Butler, there are two forms of resentment, sudden and deliberate.[25] Anger is sudden resentment, whereas deliberate resentment is resentment proper. Now it might be concluded from this that Butler held the essential difference between anger and resentment to be one of duration, but this inference would be mistaken. Rather, for Butler, the chief difference is found in the objects of these emotions. The object of resentment is moral wrongdoing, whereas the object of anger is nonmoral injury or harm. Butler puts it this way:

> But from this [sudden anger], deliberate anger or resentment is essentially distinguished, as the latter is not naturally excited by, or intended to prevent mere harm without appearance of wrong or injustice.[26]

Or again:

> From hence it appears, that it is not natural, but moral evil; it is not suffering, but injury, which raises that anger or resentment, which is of any continuance. The natural object of it is not one, who appears to the suffering person to have been only the innocent occasion of his pain or loss; but one, who has been in a moral sense injurious either to ourselves or others.[27]

To see that resentment is anger directed at moral injury, Butler argues, we need only attend to the circumstances that heighten or lessen this emotion. These, he says, are obvious. They are the same circumstances that aggravate or lessen the fault: "friendship, and former obligations, on one hand; or inadvertency, strong temptations, and mistake, on the other."[28] Indeed, he continues, consider how resentment is generally in proportion "to the degree of design and deliberation in the injurious person." This proportion is due, Butler argues, to the connection design and deliberation have to considerations of justice.

I think Butler is essentially correct here. Anger is related to resentment as genus is to species. Resentment is anger generated by and directed toward redressing an injury that is perceived as morally wrong. Where anger is an accusation of undeserved harm; resentment is an accusation of grave wrongdoing. Moreover, Butler highlights the way in which both emotions are essentially connected to what he calls "the administration of justice." In his sermon on resentment, Butler asks why God would implant in humans an emotion, like resentment, that appears so contrary to that of benevolence. The answer, he says, is that God wanted "to prevent and to remedy injury. . . . It [resentment] is to be considered as a weapon, put into our hands by nature, against injury, injustice and cruelty."[29]

If we put aside Butler's assumptions about providential design, we can see, nonetheless, that Butler is on to an important point here. Butler's comments underscore the connection in our culture between the emotions of anger and resentment and an understanding of the world that emphasizes the place of justice and individual rights. We can see that the experiences of anger and resentment are tied to a particular understanding of ourself and our world, one that attaches fundamental importance to an individual's right to make specific claims on others for his or her due. In our earlier example, when Kevin is angered by the actions of his neighbors, he is expressing his concern that his neighbors are not giving him his due. His anger is likely to be the greater, the more he focuses on how his "rights" have been violated. If Kevin focuses on the fact that the ball is on his property, and that he has a right to this property which is violated when the boys appear to retrieve their ball, he may well become even angrier.

The connection between our particular (moral) self-understanding and emotion is even clearer in the case of resentment. Tom resents the treatment he receives precisely because he believes it is unjust. He knows that he is not receiving the respect that, on his view of morality, he deserves as a fellow human being, and this realization kindles his resentment. Had he not expected to be treated with respect, had this not been a fundamental expectation on his world view, the emotion of resentment may well have been absent.[30]

That there is this connection between the retributive emotions of anger and resentment and a concern for justice and individual rights is supported by the fact that there appear to be cultures where this concern is absent and where anger is almost nonexistent. One example of such a culture, it seems, is the Utkuhikhalingmiut (Utku) Eskimos of the Northwest Territories in Canada. According to the anthropologist Jean Briggs, who lived among the Utku for nearly a year and a half, the Utku rarely get angry.[31] Further, she claims that the absence of anger is not due merely to repression; it is not simply that the Utku do not express the anger they have—although she makes it clear that the expression of anger is socially unacceptable—but that they just do not often get angry. In the Utku world, anger is a childish emotion, and the Utku were frequently amused by the fact that Professor Briggs was so easily angered. In fact, they often treated her as if she were a child because of this trait. This is significant because, according to Professor Briggs, part of what distinguishes children from adults (i.e., those who get angry from those who don't) in Utku society is that children have not yet learned one of the central concepts of Utku culture (*ayuqnaq*), what Briggs defines as fatalism, "an attitude of resignation to the inevitable."³² According to Briggs, this concept is fundamentally constitutive of the Utku world view and is repeatedly invoked by the Utku in all types of contexts.

The significance of this point can be brought out by the contrast between a world view based on *ayuqnaq* and our own. Robert Solomon has put this point quite nicely. Commenting on Briggs's observation that the Utku find the ideas of white people strange, Solomon reflects on which ideas are found strange:

> The answer started to become evident to observer Briggs from her first weeks in the Territory, our idea that a person ought to react to offenses in an aggressive way, "stand up for our rights" we would say. But this notion of "rights" is something to be understood, for it in turn reflects a certain view of the universe. It is a bourgeois view, in a sense, that the universe *owes* us an (unreasonably) high level of comfort and convenience. When we suffer discomfort or inconvenience, we blame whoever can be held *responsible*, even the universe itself ("cursing the heavens," condemning *everything*). These notions of "blame" and "right" are built into our world view. . . . The Utku, [by contrast] much more than any of us, are used to extreme hardship and discomfort. Their philosophy, therefore, is that such things must be tolerated, not flailed against. . . . In our society, the encouraged attitude, and consequently our behavior is to fight, even for a lost cause, to take up a lost cause, to take up or assign responsibility with moral enthusiasm. We are very judgmental and quick to blame. But the Utku find this idea "strange," to say the least; in fact, they think it "childish."³³

Because we are judgmental and quick to blame, anger and resentment have a prominent place in our culture. By contrast, for the Utku, there is no reason to blame because certain things just cannot be helped; one must resign oneself to the inevitable. The upshot is that anger and resentment have little place in Utku culture. The web of experience and belief that defines their world and their self-understanding just does not afford anger and resentment a prominent role in the emotional life of the community.

We have seen that anger and resentment are embedded in complex webs of descriptive and normative judgments, that these emotions are indeed constituted in community. We have seen, for example, how the experience of "anger" in Taita culture is very different from that in our own culture, and we have seen how, for the Utku, "anger" has almost no social location at all. Here, then, our previous discussion of the significance of self-understanding is joined, for our examination of anger in each of these cultures reveals how important our understanding of ourself and our world is to our emotional life. Each of these examples is thus also suggestive for our central interest, namely, the role of religious faith in shaping emotional experience. What these examples point to is how determinative a community of belief and practice can be to our emotions. This is a point we turn to in our final chapter, where we explore how the experience of anger and resentment can be different, not only in a different culture, but within a different community of discourse in our own culture.

5

Religious Belief and Emotional Transformation

We set out to explore the relationship between religious faith and emotional experience and discovered that to understand this connection we had to account for the nature of emotion and its relation to the self. We saw that emotions are best understood as complex experiences constructed and governed by social norms. We also saw that this meant that emotions are intimately connected to self-understanding and that, as a result, emotions will vary from culture to culture. We observed how this was true of the emotions of anger and resentment, and we saw in particular that in our culture the emotions of anger and resentment are experienced against the backdrop of a moral scheme that emphasizes individual rights and claims of justice. We have now to ask how these various observations work together to provide us with an answer to our guiding question: In what way or ways are emotions generated, shaped, and sustained by religious belief and practice?

To answer this question we may focus on our examples of anger and resentment. In what way or ways are anger and resentment generated, shaped, and sustained by religious belief and practice? Are we now in a position to answer this question adequately? I think that we are, and I want to begin to answer this question by examining some of the ways in which particular Christian beliefs and practices may work, not to generate and sustain anger and resentment—though that is also a possibility—but to eliminate (or mute) these emotions. That Christianity has often sought to transform anger and resentment in this fashion is evident in the claim—also found frequently in the tradition—that forgiveness is a duty. Forgiveness is generally understood in our culture to involve the elimination of anger and resentment. If this is the case, to say that forgiveness is a duty is also to say that one has an obligation not to be angry and resentful. This in turn requires that some provision be made for the transformation or elimination of anger and resentment. Thus,

91

if we can see how forgiveness might come to be understood as a duty, and how particular Christian beliefs might make forgiveness a realistic emotional possibility, we will have made considerable progress toward answering our question. Let us turn, then, to consider the experience of forgiveness.

Forgiveness as the Elimination of Anger and Resentment

When we turn to sketch an account of forgiveness, we discover that it shares one of its most striking features with the emotions of anger and resentment, namely, it too has its home in a framework of retributive justice. Forgiveness is most frequently understood in our culture by analogy with the legal categories of pardon and mercy, and it is worth looking briefly at the similarities here, for they reveal how completely forgiveness is embedded in a retributive framework.[1] Perhaps the most common feature these concepts share is the element of foregoing a claim. Mercy, pardon, and forgiveness all have their place in a situation where, as the result of offense or injury, the right to exact a claim has been created. A judge shows mercy to a first-time offender by reducing the sentence that could rightfully be applied by law; a governor pardons by releasing the convict from the penalty of an offense; a person forgives by relinquishing his or her right to resentment and retaliation in response to injury. This first shared feature suggests a second: none of the three can be claimed as a right. Just as a criminal cannot demand a light sentence or a convict a release, an offender cannot demand a reconciliation.

Both of these points suggest that the most appropriate metaphor for understanding the similarities among pardon, mercy, and forgiveness may well be that of a debt. Whether it be by injuring a person or by violating a network of institutional rules, a person creates a debt; he or she then owes, depending on the case, an apology, restitution, or a stint in jail, but the important point is that something is owed. Forgiveness, pardon, and mercy, then, can all be understood by analogy to the cancellation of a debt. Just as canceling a debt involves freely foregoing some legitimate claim, so too do forgiveness, pardon, and mercy.

So forgiveness, pardon, and mercy share a retributive framework; that is, each of these concepts presupposes the existence of a network of rights, the violation of which creates a claim. Nevertheless, forgiveness is also different from pardon and mercy. It is different because pardon and mercy presuppose an *institutional* network of rights in the form of a legal system, whereas forgiveness does not. In this respect, the fact that I earlier used the particular formulations "a governor pardons" and "a person forgives" was not accidental for a governor pardons in his or her role as an official of the legal order. By contrast, we forgive, not as members of a legal order, but as persons who have been morally wronged.[2] This leads us to another difference between forgiveness and mercy or pardon: forgiveness necessarily involves a context of interpersonal relations in which a moral relation between individuals is at stake. This is why forgiveness is generally understood to be between a victim and his or her offender—something that is not generally true of mercy or pardon—and why repentance is generally thought to be an important condition of forgiveness.

This last point is important and points to another significant difference between forgiveness and pardon or mercy. Contrition on the part of the offender is of consequence because forgiveness is not merely the cancellation of a debt—it is also the restoration of a damaged relationship. Unlike an appeal for pardon or mercy, an appeal for forgiveness is not simply a request that a rightful claim to retribution be forgone. It is also an appeal for a return to the moral *status quo ante*. This is why remorse on the part of the offender is important. It is also something that distinguishes forgiveness from pardon or mercy. Because forgiveness is appropriate in contexts where there exist relations between persons perceived as moral equals, and because the injury that generates the need for forgiveness often causes a breach in these relationships, the appeal for forgiveness is more than an appeal for nonretribution. It is a request to have a damaged relationship restored. Forgiveness, it might be said, is the effort to restore wholeness to a broken relationship, and in this it is fundamentally different from pardon and mercy. Forgiveness is essentially restorative; mercy and pardon are essentially palliative.

If we define forgiveness primarily in terms of the elimination of anger and resentment, I think we can see why forgiveness is both similar to and different from pardon and mercy in the ways we have just seen. We recall that resentment is, among other things, a retributive emotion generated by the judgment that moral harm has been done and directed toward resolving that harm. Conceiving of forgiveness as the elimination of resentment thus allows us to appreciate how forgiveness can involve both the elimination of a debt and a movement in the direction of restoration. On the one hand, because resentment is appropriate only where a person has been injured by another in violation of some standard of morality, there is a sense in which the elimination of resentment involves freely relinquishing a moral claim on the offender. On the other hand, because action consistent with the emotion of resentment should be directed toward remedying the damage done by an injury, and because the emotion itself can stand in the way of repairing one significant part of the damage, namely, the breach in a relationship, the elimination of resentment is often the first step toward the restoration of a broken relationship.

With these two features of forgiveness in mind, let us define forgiveness as follows. Forgiveness is the elimination of the retributive responses of anger and resentment in the face of moral injury and the restoration of a broken relationship following the elimination of these retributive emotions. Let us now turn to see how anger and resentment might be transformed within a religious community where forgiveness was understood to be a duty.

Self-Understanding, Anger, and Forgiveness

A key to understanding how this transformation might take place is provided by returning to the importance of self-understanding to our emotions. We saw earlier how Stanley Hauerwas's work demonstrates the importance of self-understanding to the moral life of the believer and, once again, Hauerwas's work is instructive. In a footnote to an assertion that Christians are distinct from the world in that they are required to live the life of the forgiven, Hauerwas writes:

> The command to forgive our enemies should surely be the most provocative reminder of how misleading is the claim that Christian ethics is human ethics. Human ethics is built on the assumption of the legitimacy of self-defense—as are also most accounts of natural law ethics that legitimate survival as the source of moral principles. On the other hand, Christian ethics severely qualifies that "desire." (PK, 161)

Hauerwas's comments here are extremely suggestive. They direct us to consider the prospect that Christian faith may transform the emotions of anger and resentment by transforming our understanding of ourselves and our world in such a way that anger and resentment themselves simply become less legitimate. By providing categories of self-understanding that will not legitimate self-defense, Christian faith leaves behind the retributive framework that generates and sustains anger and resentment, and that makes forgiveness a necessity. Thus, when Hauerwas writes that "human ethics is built on the assumption of the legitimacy of self-defense," he draws our attention to the fact that the emotions of anger and resentment and the experience of forgiveness are indeed, in our culture, framed against the backdrop of a moral scheme which attaches fundamental importance to the notions of justice and individual rights. Change this scheme and you will change these emotions.

To see just how this sort of transformation might take place, we need to consider the presuppositions about human nature and human history embedded in this retributive framework. In contemporary Western thought, these presuppositions emerge most clearly in discussions of what have come to be known as the "circumstances of justice."[3] The most succinct statement of these presuppositions is found in Hume. "I have already observed," Hume writes:

that justice takes its rise from human conventions; and that these are intended as a remedy to some inconveniences, which proceed from the concurrence of certain qualities of the human mind with the situation of external objects. The qualities of the mind are selfishness and limited generosity, and the situation of external objects is their easy change, join'd to their scarcity in comparison of the wants and desires of men.[4]

In so far as the "circumstances of justice" are understood to structure human social interaction, one assumes that the human condition is characterized on the one hand by limited resources, and on the other by limited generosity. Under these conditions, a framework of retributive justice will appear natural. Since individuals are regarded as threats to one another's competing interests, the existence of fences, in the form of rights, duties, and obligations, to protect these interests will go unquestioned. It is clear that this general framework stands in the background of our discussions of anger, resentment, and forgiveness. We have seen, for example, that resentment is a retributive response to moral injury and that forgiveness is the forbearance of a claim generated by such an injury. This way of understanding forgiveness presupposes that, on the one hand, one has a right not to be injured and, on the other, that the violation of that right in turn creates a claim.

We can now appreciate just how instrumental anger and resentment are to maintaining this framework of retributive justice, and how the social norms structuring anger and resentment function to accomplish this task. We saw in the last chapter that anger and resentment are socially constructed responses to the perception of intentional harm. We also saw that, in our culture, there are in fact social expectations that anger will be the response to intentional harm and that such anger will lead an individual to seek redress or to punish or both. Moreover, we discovered that there are social expectations that such anger be proportionate to the harm done and be given up when the harm is redressed. We thus discover a fascinating dialectic: the social norms governing anger and resentment both presuppose a framework of retributive justice and serve to perpetuate it.

Suppose, however, that a community of belief and practice provided an alternative conceptualization of human life. Suppose, that is, that religious belief provided a challenge not only to certain beliefs held within a moral framework which emphasizes the "circumstances of justice," but also to beliefs about the moral framework itself. I hope it is now clear that, under such circumstances, we would expect to find that the emotions of anger and resentment would themselves be changed. Just as we would not expect the experience of "anger" to be the same in Taita culture—where it is understood to be a mystically dangerous force—as in our own—where it is not so understood—so we would not expect "anger" to be the same where the circumstances of justice provide a natural home for this emotion and where the circumstances of justice are thought not to hold. Or, again, recall how the Ilongot people of the Philippines experience "anger" differently from us precisely because they do not have the conceptual framework within which to make sense of anger as a pressure that builds up inside oneself. Much the same point can be made here. If the retributive framework which generates and sustains anger and resentment is significantly changed, we cannot expect the experience of these emotions to remain the same.

To see how religious belief might effect such a change, I want to consider three ways in which the framework of retributive justice may in fact be transformed in relation to religious belief, through a transformation of an individual's self-understanding. By examining how religious faith might thus change an individual's understanding of himself and his world, we will begin to see how religious faith may transform our emotions. For convenience, let us label the three types of transformations as justice transformed, justice transferred, and justice transcended.

Justice Transformed

The first and least radical type of transformation is that in which religious faith underwrites a revision in an individual's conception of the good. In this type of transformation, the social norms governing the experiences of anger and resentment themselves remain unchanged as does the retributive framework in which these norms have their place. In Butler's words, resentment still serves the "administration of justice." Instead, how the norms are applied is changed. In other words, anger and resentment are still understood to be an appropriate response to injury; it is still socially unacceptable for them to be excessively disproportionate, they should still be given up when the harm has been adequately redressed. But what counts as "harm," "disproportionate," and "adequate" are now seen quite differently in relation to a new and different vision of human life.

Consider, for example, how our conception of "harm" may be changed. Recall that we have thus far worked with a very general conception of harm in order to be able to account for the wide variety of occasions for anger. We have seen that "harm" is generally understood in relation to our interests. One is harmed when one suffers as the result of physical injury, frustration of desires, or disregard of the goods one values, i.e., when one's interests are harmed. We saw in chapter 4, for example, that Kevin's anger would probably be sanctioned as justifiable because the goods he values have been intentionally (and for no good reason) disregarded. But "harm" could be understood quite differently. One could, for example, adopt a different measure of harm. Instead of understanding the frustration of desire as harmful, one might come to view this as relatively unimportant and in no way harmful. In other words, in relation to particular religious beliefs about human life and history, one might cease to place importance on the realization of one's desires and thus cease to care about the frustration of those desires that previously generated such anger.

This is a point that James Gustafson seems to have in mind when he discusses what he calls the "Christian sense of gratitude." Experiencing gratitude to a God who freely gives life to us as a gift, Gustafson says, leads us to reevaluate the importance of our own interests. "If ones's basic theological perception is of a Deity who rules all of creation," Gustafson writes, "then the good that God values must be more inclusive than one's normal perceptions of what is good for me, what is good for my community, and even what is good for the human species."[5] Although Gustafson is making a slightly different point from that I am trying to convey, it follows from what he says that one's perceptions of what is injurious or harmful will likewise be changed. Injury or harm will no longer be defined solely in relation to my interests, those of my community, or even those of my species. In Gustafson's language, harm will now be defined not simply as damage to an individual—though it may include that—but damage to God's created order.

This point has sometimes been expressed in the claim that the good person cannot be harmed. What lies behind this claim is the conviction that what is truly harmful is not the same as what is conventionally understood to be harmful. What counts as truly harmful is here defined in relation to a revised conception of the good. The state of one's soul (Socrates), of one's will (Kant), or of one's relation to God (many theistic believers) is now the standard by which "harm" is measured. One cannot be harmed on these criteria by the same things or in the same way as on other criteria.

Yet, if this is the case, it follows from what we have said above that the experiences of anger and resentment will not be the same, for the norms governing these experiences will be changed as well. On the one hand, anger and resentment should be less prominent because the occasions of genuine harm will be reduced. On the other hand, anger and resentment should be less intense because the harms to which they should be proportionate responses will be considered less grave.

Justice Transferred

The second type of transformation I wish to discuss involves a change, not merely in the application of the norms regarding anger and resentment, but in the demand, implicit in these norms, that we be the agents of justice. This was a thesis central to Butler's account of resentment. As Butler put it, resentment serves the administration of justice. The assumption that we serve justice through our resentment also appears to be incorporated into the social norms governing anger and resentment. We have seen, for example, that anger and resentment are properly directed toward redressing the injury and harm, and implicitly involve a sort of accusation of wrong-doing. Anger and resentment thus serve a social function; they serve as an assertion of one's claim to justice. One demands justice, as it were, through one's anger and resentment. Hence we become agents of justice, so to speak, through our anger and resentment.

Yet, the belief that we ought to be agents of justice can be changed by religious belief just as one's conception of the good may be. Just as one may revise one's understanding of injury and harm, so, too, one may come to a different understanding of what one should do when one has been injured or harmed. This is precisely the sort of change in self-understanding that Hauerwas believes Christian convictions effect. According to Hauerwas, Christian faith rejects the claim made by Butler that we are responsible for administering justice. The story of Jesus' death and resurrection, Hauerwas tells us, frees us from the "assumption that we must be in control of history, that it is up to us to make things come out right" (PK, 87). It is precisely this assumption, however, that underlies Butler's discussion of resentment and its connection with the pursuit of justice for as we have seen, Butler assumes that we are the agents of justice and that resentment facilitates its pursuit. By contrast, to use Hauerwas's words, once we abandon the assumption that "man rather than God controls the world," we will see that "the service Christians are called upon to provide does not have as its aim to make the world better, but to demonstrate that Jesus has made possible a new world" (CC, 49). We see here the sort of change in self-understanding that may well underwrite a change in one's emotional life. If one does not understand oneself to be an agent of justice, if the pursuit of justice is not a fundamental concern of the community of which one is a part, neither will resentment be understood as an emotion that must be sustained. This, as we have seen, is just what Hauerwas argues. In Hauerwas's words, the community formed by the story of Jesus' death and resurrection is both a forgiven and a forgiving community. Unlike communities not shaped by this story, the Christian community is not built on fear and resentment, and fear and resentment have little or no place in it. "The power that comes from trusting in truth," he writes:

is but a correlative of our learning through Jesus to accept our life as a gift. In Jesus we have met the one who has the authority and power to forgive our fevered search to gain security through deception, coercion, and violence. To learn to follow Jesus means we must learn to accept such forgiveness, and it is no easy thing to accept, as acceptance requires a recognition of our sin as well as vulnerability. But by learning to be forgiven we are enabled to view other lives not as threats but as gifts. *Thus in contrast to all societies built on shared resentments and fears, Christian community is formed by a story that enables its members to trust the otherness of the other as the very sign of the forgiving character of God's Kingdom.* (CC, 50)

The Christian community can afford to heal its wounds and to eliminate resentment, because God will see that justice is done. Fear and resentment may not be eliminated in such a community, but it is hoped that they will not long be sustained. I am suggesting here that the social norms governing anger and resentment will be different in a community that accepts a view of self and world set out by Hauerwas, and that such a view may well promote the elimination of anger and resentment in the form of forgiveness. Where anger and resentment are not understood to be necessary in the pursuit of justice, they will not serve the same social function.

It should be clear now why I called this type of transformation justice transferred for we can now see that, given certain beliefs about divine justice, resentment may be understood to play a very different role in human life. Where resentment was understood to be a socially acceptable response to moral injury because it served the administration of justice, it may now become socially unacceptable because the administration of justice is now thought to be God's responsibility, not our own. This is not to say that the administration of justice has become unimportant or that the framework of justice has been transcended. Moral harm is still recognized and righteous retribution is still expected, but the responsibility for retaliation is, so to speak, transferred to God. In any event, I believe that this is the best way to understand Hauerwas's claim that it is God, not humans, who controls history. This claim underscores the idea that it is God who accepts ultimate responsibility for human life. We are thus freed to give up our resentment, to forgive with the confidence that God will see that justice is done. We have now to consider the type of transformation in which the framework of justice is itself transcended, where the circumstances of justice are no longer thought to apply.

Justice Transcended

So far we have seen two ways in which particular Christian beliefs can affect the social norms structuring the experiences of anger and resentment. On the one hand, these beliefs can lead to a respecification of the norms such that what counts as "harm," "redress," "grave," etc., is redefined; on the other, they can lead to a revision in our understanding of the role anger and resentment play in the moral life and hence of their social location. Both types of change create the potential for a dramatic change in the emotional life of the believer. There remains a third type of transformation, however, that offers the potential for an even greater alteration here. If with the first type of transformation, the play remains the same but the cues change, and if with the second the play remains the same but the actors change, with the third type of transformation we have an entirely different play.

The best way to understand this type of transformation, I think, is to construe it as an extreme development or extension of the first type of transformation. Let me illustrate this point by reference to our earlier example of the redefinition of harm. We saw before that a conception of human life as a gift—together with the other beliefs that go along with it—can lead to a specification of what counts as harm which is very different from that where human life is not so conceived. It is also possible that understanding human life as a gift can lead to the adoption of a set of values in comparison to which the goods provided and insured by moral norms are relatively unimportant.[6] In this case, beliefs about God and his relations to the world lead the believer to question not merely what counts as harm, but whether anything counts as harm.[7]

The significance of such a view is that it so dramatically qualifies our everyday conception of harm or injury that at least some revision of the norms governing anger and resentment is required. Either harm and injury must now be placed in scare quotes when speaking of anger and resentment as a response to "harm," in which case the social norms to this effect will be without application because no harm, in the inverted comma sense, could ever be done or harm and injury will retain their ordinary senses in the formulation of the social norms governing anger and resentment, but then the norms themselves will have to be changed to indicate that anger and resentment are not appropriate responses to the everyday experience of harm and injury. Either way, however, there is a sense in which the framework of justice has been left behind.

We have seen how Hauerwas's work illustrates the way in which concerns about justice may be transferred to God, but his work also points to a more radical type of transformation. Consider, for example, Hauerwas's discussion of the transformation viewing human life as a gift can effect. According to Hauerwas, understanding ourselves in relation to the Christian story that human life is a gift allows us to see that sin is the attempt to claim our life, "as our particular achievement," as other than a gift. Yet, when we look at our lives as an achievement, we inevitably fear that others will damage this achievement. This is why Hauerwas says that Christianity involves training in understanding the self under the category of sin. If we understand ourselves as sinners, Hauerwas argues, we will at least be in a position to try to resist the temptation to see others as threats. We will, in other words, be in a position to revise our estimation of what is truly harmful or injurious and hence of what is really threatening. Hauerwas's examples here suggest why the circumstances of justice no longer hold: threats to our possessions will no longer be considered harmful, nor will threats to our lives for life itself is a gift, not a right. The reasoning here seems to be this: if life is a gift, then we are not entitled to it; we have no claim to life or to the possessions we acquire during life. Yet, if we are not entitled to possessions, or even to life, then we cannot be said to have a right to these. Jesus' disciples, Hauerwas writes:

> are to make a radical break with security and possessions, with the customs and habits of everyday life. . . . To become followers of Jesus means that we must, like him, be dispossessed of all that we think gives us power over our own lives and the lives of others. (PK, 86)

Or again:

> For our possessions are the source of our violence. Fearing that others desire what we have, or stung by the seldom acknowledged sense that what we have we do not deserve, we seek self-deceptive justifications that mire us in patterns of injustice which can be sustained only through coercion. And of course we believe our most precious possession to be the self we have created, that we have chosen. . . . What Jesus offers is a journey, an adventure. Once undertaken, we discover that what we once held valuable, even the self, we no longer count as anything. (PK, 86–87)

Here we see a more radical revision of a believer's understanding of herself and her circumstances. Understanding our lives as gifts and ourselves as sinners leads to a revision, not just of the role anger and resentment are thought to play in the moral life, or merely to a reduction in the number of occasions for which anger and resentment would be appropriate; rather it leads to a sort of eclipse of anger and resentment. Only when I have made the story of God my own story, Hauerwas writes, "can I learn to accept what has happened to me (which includes what I have done) without resentment." (PK, 148)

Hauerwas is in effect suggesting that Christian convictions can help form a community, similar to the Utku, in which the categories of self-understanding are such that the emotions of anger and resentment have no real foothold in the emotional life of the community. Where, for the Utku, anger and resentment have no place because one should resign oneself to one's fate, for the Christian community that accepts the view embraced by Hauerwas, anger and resentment should have no place because one does not accept the retributive framework that emerges when human life is considered to be a right rather than a gift. In other words, when one understands human life as a gift, the framework of justice is transcended and so (possibly) too, the emotions of anger and resentment.

Regardless of whether Hauerwas's vision of Christian existence is acceptable, I hope his claims about the potential for an emotional transformation are now plausible. We have seen the precise sense in which, to use the language of chapter 3, the web of belief generating and sustaining our emotional life, may be affected by a religious vision of the world. We have seen, for example, three ways in which the social norms governing anger and resentment may be transformed—a change that would quite likely result in an emotional transformation in the life of the believer.

If, then, our discussion of the social norms governing anger and resentment has been plausible, and if anger and resentment may be transformed in the ways I have just suggested, we have the beginnings of the very thing for which we have been searching: a plausible account of how Christian beliefs can have the sort of transformational effects Christian ethicists have often claimed for them.

To demonstrate that our discussion does indeed shed light on the claims made by Christian ethicists about the transforming power of faith, let us return to the claim that Christian faith both enables and requires believers to forgive unconditionally, to forgive enemies as well as friends, to forgive the unrepentant as well as the repentant. Since I believe that this claim is at odds with what is ordinarily expected of us emotionally in response to injury, in the next section of this chapter I try to show how our previous discussion of possible changes in the social norms structuring anger and resentment sheds light on this contrast. We will discover that our previous discussion allows us to appreciate how, given certain religious beliefs, forgiveness may be understood to be a duty, whereas, in a community without these beliefs, forgiveness will at best be thought of as a moral prerogative.

We can begin to see how sharp the contrast is between a view of forgiveness that understands it as a duty and (what I think is) our ordinary understanding by noting that there are circumstances in which most of us would say that forgiveness is not only not a duty, but is, on the contrary, morally problematic. Aurel Kolnai, for example, has tried to highlight the problematic character of forgiveness by setting out what he calls the logical paradox of forgiveness. Kolnai explains the paradox this way. When we forgive someone:

> Either the wrong is still flourishing, the offence still subsisting: then by "forgiving" you accept it and thus confirm it and make it worse; or the wrongdoer has suitably annulled and eliminated his offence, and then by harping on it further you would set up a new evil and by "forgiving" you would only acknowledge the fact that you are no longer its victim. Briefly, forgiveness is either unjustified or pointless.[8]

I hope it is clear from my earlier sketch of a paradigm of forgiveness that I do not share Kolnai's view that to forgive someone who is unrepentant is merely to acknowledge that one is no longer a victim and therefore pointless. Insofar as forgiveness involves the elimination of anger and resentment and the restoration of a damaged relationship, it clearly has a point, whether the offender has repented or not. Yet precisely because it does involve overcoming anger and resentment and restoring a relationship, the first horn of Kolnai's dilemma is particularly acute. The question it raises is essentially this: Is forgiveness morally acceptable in the absence of repentance? And the answer Kolnai suggests is: "No." The problem here is that in the absence of repentance, forgiving appears equivalent to condoning, and condonation undercuts retribution. Consider what we have seen forgiveness to involve: (1) the remission of the retributive response of anger and resentment, and, following the elimination of anger and resentment (2) a reconciliation with the offender. Given the retributive framework in which forgiveness has its home, in a situation where there has been no change of heart, there is simply no reason to relinquish one's anger and resentment because the redress that is socially expected has not been forthcoming. Indeed, to give up one's anger and resentment here could well have the effect of encouraging the wrongdoing since the wrongdoer may mistake the absence of anger and resentment for a lack of concern about the objectionable behavior. Further, because the wrongdoer has not renounced his deed, to restore the relationship that existed prior to the injury would be to accept the wrongdoer *qua* offender into a relationship of moral equality, and this is tantamount to overlooking, or worse, to acquiescing to the offense. Given a framework of retributive justice, it seems that forgiveness can be morally objectionable.[9]

If we step back and examine the relation between the paradigm of forgiveness sketched above and the social norms structuring the experiences of anger and resentment, we can begin to understand why there are situations in which forgiveness will be problematic and why we do not ordinarily think of forgiveness as a duty. Because forgiveness involves the elimination of anger and resentment, we would expect our understanding of forgiveness to embody the social norms governing these emotions. We can see this to be the case. Consider, for example, how close the correspondence is between the paradigm of forgiveness I sketched and the social norms governing anger and resentment. We saw that forgiveness is an appropriate response in a situation where one individual unjustifiably injures another. In such a situation, we said, a sort of moral debt is created. The injured party can expect some sort of restitution, but should also be prepared to cease to be angry and resentful if restitution is made. It should be clear that this account of forgiveness incorporates the social norms governing anger and resentment. We saw for example that anger and resentment are responses to injury and harm, that they should be roughly proportionate to the offense, and that they should be directed to righting the wrong.

It is precisely because we do take seriously the judgments and beliefs that frame the social norms of anger and resentment that their elimination in the absence of repentance, or in the face of a particularly grave offense, is problematic, not only theoretically, but emotionally. We do believe that we deserve respect; that others should be held accountable for their actions; that the gravity of an offense is relevant to the intensity of our response; that restitution should be made for injuries and that justice should be done. Yet to demand the elimination of anger and resentment unconditionally, and to argue that forgiveness is a duty means to abandon or at least to revise these convictions in drastic fashion.

It is striking here that just these convictions are those that, in the previous section, we saw may be qualified by religious beliefs about the human situation and about divine justice. We saw, for example, that the importance of one's own interests can be downplayed (justice transformed); that justice, while important, can be left to God (justice transferred); and that the very notion of harm can lose its meaning (justice transcended).

We can now begin to see that if Christian belief can qualify these convictions, then the possibility of forgiveness being transformed in the manner claimed, for example, by Hauerwas, is a real one. For one thing, we can see how the problems that deterred us from treating forgiveness as a duty, problems connected to the social norms of anger and resentment, may be dissolved in the context of Christian faith. Where before, forgiveness in the absence of repentance was problematic, it may now not be so. Where before, forgiving in this situation meant resigning any claim to retribution and risking encouraging the wrongdoer, it may now mean only that one, so to speak, turns over the right of retribution to God. Where before, restoring a relationship with a wrongdoer *qua* offender seemed problematic, it may now not seem so, for we are all sinners, and thus relate to everyone *qua* offender. These problems are all resolved through a fundamental change in the conception of the circumstances of human existence, a change in which the circumstances of justice are transformed, transferred, or transcended. What Frederick Carney characterizes as a transvaluation of values takes place, such that, in the context of the new beliefs about God and the world, a radical devaluation of earthly goods ensues.[10] The believer both redefines his or her interests in relation to God and comes to rely on God for the provision of those interests.

The upshot of these changes however, extends beyond the mere resolution of the problems facing a characterization of forgiveness as a duty for these changes in belief underwrite another, more significant change, namely, a change in the emotional life of the believer. The beliefs embraced by someone like Hauerwas, for example, not only require forgiveness, they make it possible. They make forgiveness an emotional possibility because they lead to a revision of the judgments and beliefs which generate and sustain the emotions of anger and resentment. Where what previously counted as harm and injury no longer does so, where the believer is only provisionally concerned with the things of this world, where justice is left in the hands of God, anger and resentment may come to be, if not alien, at least less familiar emotions. Moreover, when they do occur, they will not long be sustained. In these circumstances the character of forgiveness will be very different. As we have seen, in the most radical case, where the circumstances of justice are transcended, forgiveness may have more the quality of prevention than of cure. Here, because an injury does not give rise to anger and resentment in such an individual, and thus causes no breach in a relationship, it may even be somewhat misleading to speak of forgiveness for there is no anger or resentment to be eliminated and no damaged relationship to repair. Yet, even here the believer would still be able to recognize some uncharitable bit of behavior as something at which he or she might justifiably take offense, and thus it seems appropriate to say of such a person that he or she exhibits a forgiving spirit.

The ability of Christian faith to transform the emotions of anger and resentment in this way and thus generate a forgiving spirit is very clearly and eloquently articulated by Soren Kierkegaard in his book, *Works of Love*, and we can close this chapter by attending to Kierkegaard's discussion. In a section of the work titled, "Love Builds Up," Kierkegaard discusses a situation in which the moral relations between individuals are not governed by considerations of justice. In this section Kierkegaard asks what the consequences might be of presupposing that love is fundamentally present in other people. To presuppose that love is present in others is, says Kierkegaard, what love means. Such a view of love can be expressed in the notion that "love hopes all things." According to Kierkegaard, "to hope all things means, even though love is not apparent, even though the opposite is seen, to presuppose that love is nevertheless fundamentally present and that it will show itself in the deluded, in the misguided, and even in the lost."[11] Kierkegaard continues here by noting how such a presupposition leads to a kind of forgiveness. He makes his point in connection to the biblical story of the prodigal son. "Remember," Kierkegaard writes,

> that the prodigal son's father was perhaps the only one who did not know that he had a prodigal son, for the father's love hoped all things. The brother promptly saw that he [the prodigal son] was hopelessly lost. . . . In spite of the son's misguided conduct *there was no break on the father's side* (a break is just the opposite of building up); he hoped all things; therefore he in truth built up through his fatherly forgiveness, since the son vividly grasped the fact that fatherly love had carried through with him and that there had been no break.[12]

Kierkegaard's point here is that the father's emotional life has been changed by his belief that even in the deluded, the misguided, and the lost, love is still present. Unlike his second son, the father is not angry or resentful about the actions of his prodigal son nor is he inclined to punish him in a retributive fashion. Quite the reverse: the father is overwhelmed with joy at the return of his son. This is, in fact, Kierkegaard's point, that is, the difference between the father's joyful response and the brother's angry response is to be understood in terms of the transformation of the father's emotional life brought about by the Christian conviction that love is to be presupposed in all things.

It seems to me that Kierkegaard has here captured precisely the sort of emotional transformation that religious life is capable of sustaining. We are now in a position to understand how such a transformation takes place. We can see that, in the language used above, the norms governing the experiences of anger and resentment in the father's life have been transformed in such a way that these emotions are no longer appropriate in the context of the story of the prodigal son. The father feels differently than the brother precisely because his emotional life is founded on the presupposition that love is fundamentally present in others. In other words, the model of moral relations governing the father's reaction is not one premised on the presupposition of mutual threat, but on the presupposition of mutual love. Where this is true, we have seen, the retributive emotions of anger and resentment simply do not have a home, or at least not a particularly hospitable one. As Kierkegaard puts it, the presupposition that love is fundamentally present is incompatible with "irritability and resentment."

Kierkegaard's example thus provides a nice illustration of the sort of emotional transformation for which I have been trying to account. What his example does not show, probably because the story of the prodigal son is so familiar, is how such a person as the prodigal son's father may in real life appear so very foreign to us. Here is an individual who does not respond emotionally to the same things, or in the same ways, as we do. This is why I think it is appropriate to say of such an individual that religious belief has changed the whole person for religious belief has changed, not only one's beliefs, but also one's emotions. Such persons may indeed appear mysterious to us, if only because they may appear so completely different from us emotionally. But to say that such persons may seem mysterious is not to say that the transformation by which their emotions came to differ from our own is itself a mystery. On the contrary, if what I have argued in chapters 1 through 4 is correct, then we have a detailed and, I think, plausible account of how religious belief can transform the whole person. If emotions are in fact interpretations of experience governed by social norms, and if, as I have repeatedly urged, they have their place in a web of belief and judgment about the world, then they can be radically transformed in the face of revised assumptions about self and world provided by religious belief. This is why the notion of self-understanding must play such a crucial role in any explication of the relation of religious faith to moral experience. Self-understanding embodies those beliefs about the self and the world that give substance and coherence to our emotional lives.

Change self understanding, and the possibility of a tremendous emotional transformation is generated. My hope is that our discussion of human emotions and their relation to self-understanding has shed light on the possibility of a religious transformation of emotional life more generally. I hope, that is, that this study has enabled us to see what it might mean to say that religious faith may light a candle of understanding in one's heart.

Conclusion

The immediate concern of this study has been to provide an account of one of the ways in which Christian belief can affect the moral life of the believer. Throughout, my goal has been to offer a detailed and plausible explication of the claim, made by many Christian ethicists, that Christian faith can dramatically transform moral experience. I have tried to show that claims about the effects Christian faith can have on the moral life, as well as the effects themselves, cannot be fully understood without taking account of the importance of our emotions. In pursuing this goal, however, we quickly discovered that a proper reckoning of our emotions required that we attend to the significance of self-understanding to our emotional life and that this, in turn, required abandoning the traditional dichotomy between reason and emotion.

This realization led us to reconsider the traditional view of emotions and to sketch an alternative theory of emotion. We discovered that emotions are best understood, not as irrational, biologically primitive forces, but as meaningful experiences embedded in social practices. Viewing emotions in this way enabled us to see the emotions of anger and resentment in a new light. In particular, we saw that anger and resentment are cognitively structured experiences which have their place within a framework that emphasizes individual rights and human justice. We also saw that this framework may be revised, and even abandoned, in the face of particular Christian beliefs. Most importantly, though, we saw how and why such a revision, or desertion, of this framework affects the emotions of anger and resentment by altering the social norms structuring these emotions. We saw that specific Christian beliefs about human life and history may provide for a fundamentally different self-understanding, one which underwrites a change in the emotional life of the believer. The beliefs that life is a gift from God, that God is responsible for seeing that justice is done, and that in comparison to the importance of our relationship to God nothing else matters significantly alter the conditions in which the emotions of anger and resentment are generated and sustained. The upshot of this alteration is that the emotions of anger and resentment may become much less prominent, perhaps even absent.

With the detailed account in chapter 5 of how this sort of transformation is possible, we realized the central goal of this study. We had asked at the start: "In what way or ways are emotions generated, shaped, and sustained by religious belief and practice?" We answered this question by showing how emotions are embedded in social practices and changed when the beliefs shaping these practices are themselves revised. We saw how this was true of anger and resentment. Nevertheless, I hope that the significance of this study is not restricted simply to the light it sheds on how specific Christian beliefs can affect the particular emotions of anger and resentment. The general point of this study is that understanding emotions as meaningful experiences governed by social norms opens the possibility of understanding the role Christian faith can have in shaping a whole range of emotional experience. That Christian faith can generate and sustain emotions of hope, compassion, gratitude, and joy, among others, is a claim often touted by Christian writers.[1] We are now in a position to see that this is not empty and wishful bravado. When emotions are understood as socially governed experiences which are, to use Solomon's words again, "part of an elaborate web of experience and belief," we can begin to appreciate how Christian belief might generate the emotions of hope, compassion, or gratitude. Since Christian faith may contribute importantly to the construction of the webs of experience and belief of which we have repeatedly spoken, it follows that Christian belief may play a role in developing the emotions supported by these webs. We have seen in some detail how this may happen in the case of anger and resentment. It would be a valuable extension of this study to examine how Christian beliefs may shape emotions other than anger and resentment.

If this study has demonstrated that the claim that Christian faith can shape one's emotions is not a vain boast, it should also have demonstrated that this is an achievement scarcely unique to Christianity. This points us to a second direction in which this study might usefully be extended. Not only has this study laid the groundwork for a detailed examination of the relation between Christian beliefs and a whole range of human emotions, it has also provided a foundation for the claim that any religious system can shape emotions in important and distinctive ways. This has been a claim expressed tacitly throughout this study, and it is one worth articulating explicitly in closing. Although we have focused on the way in which specific Christian beliefs can shape one's emotions, it should be clear by now that any system of belief and practice has the potential for generating and sustaining particular emotions. Indeed, we are now in a position to understand precisely what Clifford Geertz meant when he said that there exists a dialectical relationship between a group's world view and their emotions. Given the close connection we have noted between emotions and self-understanding, it could not be otherwise.

We have seen how this dialectic operates in the case of anger and resentment, how anger and resentment are ordered and defined in relation to our own culture's views about injury, rights, claims of justice, about emotions in general, and in the Christian's case, about God's role in human life and history. We have also seen, in the case of the Taita and the Utku, how a different picture of how the world ultimately is results in a very different view, and, presumably, experience of anger. There is no reason to think that this dialectical relationship is limited to these examples. Yet, if such a dialectic is widespread, then the study of the relation between world views and emotions must assume a greater importance for the student of religion than it has previously. This is particularly true for the student of religious ethics, for little could be more determinative of the character of the everyday life of the believer than his or her emotions.

Emotions are central to the moral life, and emotions are inextricably tied to beliefs about ourselves and our world. These two theses have underwritten everything I have tried to do in this study. Although I believe the implications of these insights extend far beyond anything I have argued for here, if I have demonstrated the importance of these claims to understanding Christian ethics, I will have accomplished the most important goal of this study.

Notes

Works frequently cited in the text are identified by the following abbreviations:

CC   Stanley Hauerwas, *Character and the Christian Life: A Study in Theological Ethics* (San Antonio, Tex.: Trinity University Press, 1975).

GW   John Steinbeck, *The Grapes of Wrath* (New York: Viking Press, 1967).

HAL   Charles Taylor, *Human Agency and Language,* vol. 1, *Philosophical Papers of Charles Taylor* (Cambridge: Cambridge University Press, 1985).

PC   Stanley Hauerwas, *The Peaceable Kingdom* (Notre Dame, Ind.: University of Notre Dame Press, 1983).

PHS   Charles Taylor, *Philosophy and the Human Sciences,* vol. 2, *Philosophical Papers of Charles Taylor* (Cambridge: Cambridge University Press, 1985).

VV   Stanley Hauerwas, *Vision and Virtue* (Notre Dame, Ind.: Fides Publishers, 1974).

TT   Stanley Hauerwas, *Truthfulness and Tragedy* (Notre Dame, Ind.: University of Notre Dame Press, 1977).

Introduction

1. H. A. Prichard, "Does Moral Philosophy Rest on a Mistake?" in *Moral Obligation,* by H. A. Prichard, ([1912]; reprint, London: Oxford University Press, 1949), p. 12.
2. See William Frankena, "Prichard and the Ethics of Virtue—Notes on a Footnote," *Monist* 54 (1970): 1–17.
3. A similar point has been made by D. Z. Phillips in his book, *Through a Darkening Glass* (Notre Dame, Ind.: University of Notre Dame Press, 1982). Phillips puts the point in terms of a contrast of the complexity of actual moral life versus the simplicity of modern moral philosophy.
4. On the place of emotions in recent writings in feminist ethics, see my essay, "Reflections on the Nether World: Some Problems for a Feminist Ethic of Care and Compassion," forthcoming in *Soundings*.
5. James Gustafson, *Christ and the Moral Life* (New York: Harper and Row, 1968), p. 242.

6. James Gustafson, *Can Ethics Be Christian?* (Chicago: University of Chicago Press, 1975), p. 44.

7. *Ibid.,* p. 92.

8. Gustafson, *Ethics from a Theocentric Perspective,* vol. 1 (Chicago: University of Chicago Press, 1981), p. 120.

9. *Ibid.,* p. 118.

10. Alasdair MacIntyre, *After Virtue* (Notre Dame, Ind.: University of Notre Dame Press, 1981), p. 30.

11. See Charles Taylor, *Human Agency and Language* (Cambridge: Cambridge University Press, 1985).

12. I will use these two terms interchangeably, since what the natural science approach seeks is an objective or absolute account of human behavior.

13. Although a narrative view of the self is not necessarily equivalent to what Taylor calls a hermeneutical view, they share the conviction that self-understanding is determinative of our agency.

14. Taylor would argue, of course, that this picture of emotions results from adopting an objectivist approach to the study of human behavior.

15. Clifford Geertz, *The Interpretation of Cultures* (New York: Basic Books, 1973), pp. 126–41.

Chapter 1. The Place of Emotions in Religious Ethics

1. William Frankena, "The Ethics of Love Conceived as an Ethics of Virtue," *Journal of Religious Ethics* 1 (1973): 21–36.

2. Stanley Hauerwas, *Vision and Virtue* (Notre Dame, Ind.: Fides Publishers, 1974), p. 1.

3. Stanley Hauerwas, *Truthfulness and Tragedy* (Notre Dame, Ind.: University of Notre Dame Press, 1977), p. 41.

4. In his more recent writings, Hauerwas has disavowed the view that virtue and obligation pose exclusive choices. See Stanley Hauerwas, *A Community of Character* (Notre Dame, Ind.: University of Notre Dame Press, 1981) p. 98, and *The Peaceable Kingdom* (Notre Dame, Ind.: University of Notre Dame Press, 1983), p. 22.

5. For a similar sort of argument, see Bernard Williams, "Persons, Character, and Morality," in his *Moral Luck* (Cambridge: Cambridge University Press, 1981).

6. Thomas Ogletree, "Character and Narrative: Stanley Hauerwas' Studies of the Christian Life," *Religious Studies Review* 6/1 (1980): 26.

7. See Ogletree's comment that this is the central question in Hauerwas's work.

8. Ogletree argues that narrative, not character, is the true center of Hauerwas's thought.

9. Mary Midgley, *Heart and Mind* (New York: St. Martin's Press, 1981), p. 5.

10. On the idea of moral self-sufficiency, see Martha Nussbaum, *The Fragility of Goodness* (Cambridge: Cambridge University Press, 1986).

11. I have developed this point more fully in "Errors of an Ill-Reasoning Reason: The Disparagement of Emotions in the Moral Life," *The Journal of Value Inquiry* (forthcoming).

12. Immanuel Kant, *Foundations of the Metaphysics of Morals,* trans. Lewis White Beck (Indianapolis, Ind.: Bobbs-Merrill, 1959), p. 10.

13. Throughout his writings, Kant draws a distinction between emotion (Affekt) and passion (Leidenschaft). For Kant, emotions are essentially spontaneous feelings that precede deliberation. As such, they are morally indifferent. By contrast, passions belong to the faculty of desire and presuppose a maxim. Hence, they are deliberate and thus pose a far greater threat to human freedom. Most of the really nasty remarks Kant makes about human emotional life are directed at passions, not emotions. He says, for example, that passions are "cancerous sores" for pure practical reason. On this distinction between emotion and passion, see Immanuel Kant, *Anthropology from a Pragmatic Point of View*, trans. Mary Gregor (The Hague: Martinus Nijhoff, 1974), esp. Book 3, and Immanuel Kant, *The Critique of Judgement*, trans. James Meredith (Oxford: Clarendon Press, 1952), esp. Book II, Part I.

14. Immanuel Kant, *Metaphysical Principles of Virtue*, trans. James Ellington (Indianapolis, Ind.: 1964; reprint, Indianapolis, Ind.: Hackett, 1983), pp. 67–68.

15. Kant, *Metaphysical Principles of Virtue*, p. 68.

16. On the role of benevolent emotions in Kant, see David Cartwright, "Kant's View of the Moral Significance of Kindhearted Emotions and the Moral Insignificance of Kant's View," *Journal of Value Inquiry* 21 (1987): 291–304.

17. For a discussion of the role of regret in such situations, see Bernard Williams's essay, "Moral Luck," in his collection of his essays by the same name (Cambridge: Cambridge University Press, 1981), pp. 20–39.

18. For a defense of the legitimacy of such attachments, see Lawrence Blum, *Friendship, Altruism. and Morality* (London: Routledge and Kegan Paul, 1980).

19. MacIntyre, *After Virtue,* p. 201.

20. *Ibid.,* pp. 205–6.

21. For an illustration of the importance of narrative to self-identity, see Oliver Sacks, *The Man Who Mistook His Wife for a Hat: And Other Clinical Tales* (New York: Harper and Row, 1970).

Chapter 2. Emotions, Self-Understanding, and Religious Ethics

1. See Charles Taylor, *Human Agency and Language* (Cambridge: Cambridge University Press, 1985), and Charles Taylor, *Philosophy and the Human Sciences* (Cambridge: Cambridge University Press, 1985). See also Taylor's most recent work, *Sources of the Self—The Making of the Modern Identity* (Cambridge: Harvard University Press, 1989).

2. Michael Sandel, *Liberalism and the Limits of Justice* (Cambridge: Cambridge University Press, 1982), p. 179.

3. Stanley Hauerwas, *The Peaceable Kingdom* (Notre Dame, Ind.: University of Notre Dame Press, 1983), p. 43.

4. Taylor is careful to indicate that he is not speaking about a necessary causal relation here. That is, I could believe that I have done something dishonorable and not feel shame, but I could not feel shame unless I was concerned about something dishonorable.

5. Thanks to Robert C. Roberts for pressing me on this point.

6. Leo Tolstoy, *The Death of Ivan Ilyich*, trans. Lynn Solotaroff (Toronto: Bantam Books, 1981), p. 93.
7. On this point, see Peter Berger, "On the Obsolescence of the Concept of Honor," in *Revisions: Changing Perspectives in Moral Philosophy,* ed. Stanley Hauerwas and Alasdair MacIntyre (Notre Dame, Ind.: University of Notre Dame Press, 1983), pp. 172–81.
8. On the relation of this point to religious experience, see Wayne Proudfoot, *Religious Experience* (Berkeley: University of California Press, 1985).
9. Taylor labels Donald Davidson's theory "neo-designative" because, although it explicates meaning in terms of truth conditions of sentences, these truth conditions are observable and thus function as extralinguistic reality on this theory. See *Human Agency and Language*, p. 243.
10. Tolstoy, *The Death of Ivan Ilyich*, p. 119; emphasis added.

Chapter 3. Toward a Constructivist Theory of Emotion

1. Actually, James offered an account of emotion that was strikingly similar to one developed by the Danish psychologist, Carl Lange. Although they arrived at their positions independently, and although there were some subtle differences between their respective accounts, the general theory became known as the James-Lange theory. I will focus exclusively on James's version, for it is James's statement of the position that has had the most influence.
2. William James, *The Varieties of Religious Experience* (New York: Collier Books, 1961), p. 337; emphasis added.
3. We may wonder whether the image conveys quite the meaning today that it did in James's own time. In our so-called postmodern age, an age in which literary criticism makes the reader "no longer the consumer but the producer of the text," as Roland Barthes has said, James's metaphor may not effectively convey his meaning. (As quoted in Jonathan Culler, *On Deconstruction* [Ithaca: Cornell University Press, 1982], p. 38.)
4. On the effects of this shift for Christian writers, see Jeffrey Stout, *The Flight from Authority* (Notre Dame, Ind.: University of Notre Dame Press, 1981).
5. On appeals to religious experience as protection for religion against the challenges of modern science, see Wayne Proudfoot, *Religious Experience* (Berkeley: University of California Press, 1985).
6. William James and Carl C. Lange, "What Is an Emotion?" in *The Emotions* (Baltimore: Williams and Wilkins, 1922), p. 13.
7. On this point, see Philip P. Wiener, *Evolution and the Founders of Pragmatism* (Cambridge: Harvard University Press, 1949).
8. Robert Solomon, *The Passions: The Myth and Nature of Human Emotions* (New York: Anchor Press, 1976), p. 141.
9. For an excellent discussion of various philosophical theories of emotion, including the so-called "feeling" theory, see William Lyons, *Emotion* (Cambridge: Cambridge University Press, 1980).
10. For a brief review of some of the literature here, see George Mandler, "Emotion,"

in *The First Century of Experimental Psychology*, ed. Eliot Hearst (Hillsdale, N.J.: Lawrence Erlbaum, 1979). We will see below that at least one strand of contemporary psychology has veered sharply away from James at this point.

11. "What Is an Emotion," pp. 13–14. This essay was originally published in the journal *Mind* in 1884. Richard Lazarus discusses the idea of genetically based triggers as a possible explanation of our fear of snakes. He argues that such triggers are not incompatible with a cognitive view of emotions. See Richard Lazarus, "Thoughts on the Relation Between Emotion and Cognition," *American Psychologist* 37/9 (1982): 1021.

12. For a discussion of these two differentia, see William Lyons's book, *Emotion* (Cambridge: Cambridge University Press, 1980), especially chapter 2. For an attempt to develop a cognitive theory that does not accept (1), see Robert C. Roberts, "What an Emotion Is: A Sketch," *Philosophical Review* 97 (1988): 183–209.

13. On this point, see Robert Gordon, "The Aboutness of Emotions," *American Philosophical Quarterly* 11 (1974): 27–36.

14. Again, for a brief review of the literature, see Mandler.

15. See Stuart Hampshire, "Sincerity and Single-Mindedness," in *Freedom of Mind and Other Essays* (Princeton, N.J.: Princeton University Press, 1971).

16. Hampshire, "Sincerity and Single-Mindedness," p. 241.

17. *Ibid.,* p. 244.

18. Clifford Geertz, *The Interpretation of Cultures* (New York: Basic Books, 1973), p. 37.

19. Geertz, *The Interpretation of Cultures*, p. 49.

20. *Ibid.,* p. 50.

21. In philosophy, see William Lyons, *Emotion* (Cambridge: Cambridge University Press, 1980); Amélie Rorty, ed. , *Explaining Emotions* (Berkeley: University of California Press, 1980); Robert Solomon, *The Passions: The Myth and Nature of Human Emotions* (New York: Anchor Press, 1976); and Charles Taylor, *Human Agency and Language* and *Philosophy and the Human Sciences* (Cambridge: Cambridge University Press, 1985). In psychology, see James Averill, *Anger and Aggression: An Essay on Emotion* (New York: Springer-Verlag, 1982); Richard Lazarus, "On the Primacy of Cognition," *American Psychologist* 39 (1984): 124–29; and Klaus Scherer and Paul Ekman, ed. , *Approaches to Emotion* (Hillsdale, N.J.: Lawrence Erlbaum, 1984).

22. See Michelle Rosaldo, "Toward an Anthropology of Self and Feeling," in *Culture Theory*, ed. Richard A. Shweder and Robert A. LeVine (Cambridge: Cambridge University Press, 1984). See also Catherine A. Lutz, *Unnatural Emotions—Everyday Sentiments on a Micronesian Atoll and Their Challenge to Western Theory* (Chicago: University of Chicago Press, 1988).

23. On the idea of anger as a commodity in our culture, see Arlie Hochschild, *The Managed Heart* (Berkeley: University of California Press, 1983).

24. Rosaldo, "Toward an Anthropology," p. 146.

25. *Ibid.,* p. 150.

26. *Ibid.,* p. 143.

27. Robert Solomon, "Emotions and Anthropology: The Logic of Emotional World Views," *Inquiry* 21 (1978): 187.

28. Robert Solomon, "Paul Ricoeur on Passion and Emotion," in *Studies in the Philosophy of Paul Ricoeur*, ed. Charles E. Reagan (Athens: Ohio University Press, 1979), p. 19.

29. Solomon, "Paul Ricoeur," p. 19.

30. James Averill, *Anger and Aggression: An Essay on Emotion* (New York: Springer-Verlag, 1982). See also Arlie Hochschild, *The Managed Heart* (Berkeley: University of California Press, 1983).

31. Averill, *Anger and Aggression*, p. 327.

32. John Searle, *Speech Acts* (Cambridge: Cambridge University Press, 1969).

33. *Ibid.*, p. 13.

34. *Ibid.*, p. 33.

35. *Ibid.*, pp. 34–35.

36. *Ibid.*, p. 36.

37. Peter Winch, *The Idea of a Social Science* (London: Routledge and Kegan Paul, 1958), p. 32.

38. This definition is very close to that offered by Averill, and I am in fact very indebted to Averill's treatment of emotions in this chapter.

39. The idea that cognitive components are, so to speak, the glue here is not new to me. See William Lyons, *Emotion* (Cambridge: Cambridge University Press, 1980) and Richard Lazarus, James Coyne and Susan Folkman, "Cognition, Emotion and Motivation: The Doctoring of Humpty-Dumpty," *Approaches to Emotion*, ed. Klaus Scherer and Paul Ekman (Hillsdale, N.J.: Lawrence Erlbaum, 1984).

40. Geertz, *The Interpretation of Cultures*, p. 49.

41. Ludwig Wittgenstein, *Philosophical Investigations* (New York: Macmillan, 1969), part ii, p. 174e. Or again: "'For a second he felt violent pain.' Why does it sound queer to say: 'For a second he felt deep grief'? Only because it so seldom happens?" See also the comments at part I, section 583, p. 153e.

Chapter 4. The Emotions of Anger and Resentment

1. On this point, compare Arlie Hochschild, *The Managed Heart* (Berkeley: University of California Press, 1983), and Carol Z. and Peter N. Stearns, *Anger: The Struggle for Emotional Control in America's History* (Chicago: University of Chicago Press, 1986).

2. Michel Montaigne, "Of Anger" in *The Complete Essays of Montaigne*, trans. Donald M. Frame (Stanford, Calif.: Stanford University Press, 1965), p. 540.

3. That we make this evaluation is itself significant. I will return to this point shortly.

4. One could, of course, argue that his anger is unjustified, that Kevin mistakenly values property more than concern for John or David's well being. The point I am making, however, remains the same: it makes sense to evaluate anger.

5. I am using both "harm" and "redress" as umbrella concepts for a variety of injuries, slights, offenses, and wrongs in the one case and a variety of forms of relief from injury—both compensatory and retributive—in the other.

6. There are of course cases in which it is not, strictly speaking, possible either to obtain redress or to prevent the harm from recurring. One can certainly be angry with the drunk driver who has killed one's only child, even when the drunk driver has himself died in the accident. In this case there is no real possibility of compensation, retribution, or repetition of the harm, and so anger cannot be directed toward these. Here anger is primarily an expression of the value one places on the life of one's child. I owe this example to Dan Brock.

7. I say "in part" because it is clear that the intensity of one's anger can be affected by factors other than cognitive ones. Drinking ten cups of coffee will, in all likelihood, increase the intensity of one's anger.

8. Averill argues that some of our social norms regarding anger are incorporated in our legal system. For example, in some states it is possible to defend oneself against a murder charge by invoking one's justifiable anger in some situation. The courts generally follow a "reasonable man" standard in such cases. The question in these cases becomes whether a reasonable man would have been provoked to uncontrollable rage in a particular situation.

9. See, for example, the judgment made of Achilles's treatment of Hector's corpse in the *Iliad*: "For it is senseless clay that he outrages in his wrath" (Book xxiv).

10. Robert Solomon, "Emotions and Anthropology: The Logic of Emotional World Views," *Inquiry* 21 (1978): 187.

11. It should be pointed out, however, that Freud's own views on emotions are notoriously ambiguous. It is also worth pointing out that this hydraulic model was not new with Freud; he merely dressed it up in the fashion of a science. Hence Solomon's claim: "in 'prescientific' psychology thinking the concepts of 'force' and 'energy,' 'animal spirits' and 'bodily fluids' (bile, gall, phlegm, etc.), were permitted a holiday of poetic and metaphorical explorations, consequently structuring language and thought about the passions with an unabashed and uncritical . . . hydraulic model. It quite literally views the human psyche as a caldron of pressures demanding their release in action and expression. With the advent of scientific psychology, however, the metaphor required a tangible basis, which James and Freud simultaneously located in the components of the central nervous system" (Robert Solomon, *The Passions*, p. 142).

12. Anger is here in quotation marks to highlight the fact that the emotional experience in another culture that we call anger is not necessarily the same emotion we experience.

13. Grace Gredys Harris, *Casting out Anger* (Cambridge: Cambridge University Press, 1978).

14. *Batasi* is the term by which the Taita refer to themselves.

15. Grace Gredys Harris, *Casting out Anger*, p. 78.

16. *Ibid.,* pp. 25–26. As this passage makes clear, the mystical power of the anger seems to work through the agency of certain mystical beings.

17. *Ibid.,* p. 31.

18. This way of putting it may be slightly misleading for the Taita do proscribe behavior here, only they see being angry itself as an action. It is thus the behavior of being angry which is circumscribed.

19. Harris, *Casting out Anger*, pp. 174–75.

20. John Steinbeck, *The Grapes of Wrath* (New York: The Viking Press, 1967).

21. See Robert Con Davis, ed. , *The Grapes of Wrath: A Collection of Critical Essays* (Englewood Cliffs, N. J. : Prentice Hall, 1982).

22. One of the characters explains to Tom Joad what an Okie is: "Well, Okie use'ta mean you was from Oklahoma. Now it means you're a dirty son-of-a-bitch. Okie means you're scum. Don't mean nothin itself, it's the way they say it" (280).

23. I borrow this example from Averill. See his article, "Emotion and Anxiety: Sociological, Biological, and Psychological Determinants," in *Emotions and Anxiety*, ed. M. Zuckerman and C. Spielberger (Hillsdale, N. J.: Lawrence Erlbaum, 1976), p. 106.

24. We commonly use "resentment" to refer to two distinct emotional responses: moral indignation and a sort of servile bitterness. My discussion of resentment in this chapter refers only to the former.

25. See Joseph Butler, Sermon Eight, "Upon Resentment," in *The Works of Bishop Butler* (London: Macmillan and Co. , 1900).
26. *Ibid.,* p. 105.
27. *Ibid.,* p. 106. For a similar distinction between anger and resentment see also John Rawls, *A Theory of Justice* (Cambridge: Harvard University Press, 1971), sections 73 and 74, and Michael Pritchard, "Human Dignity and Justice," *Ethics* 82 (1972): 299–313.
28. Butler, "Upon Resentment," p. 107.
29. Joseph Butler, *The Works of Bishop Butler.* p. 107.
30. I believe that William Styron explores this idea in his novel, *The Confessions of Nat Turner.* Styron portrays the uneducated and mistreated slaves around Nat Turner as incapable of genuine resentment because they do not perceive themselves as moral equals to their white owners. By contrast, Nat is consumed by righteous anger because he was raised in the owner's house and treated as equal. His resentment is generated when he is once again treated as a slave.
31. Jean L. Briggs, *Never in Anger—Portrait of an Eskimo Family* (Cambridge: Harvard University Press, 1970).
32. On this point, see Robert Solomon's discussion of Briggs's book in "Emotions and Anthropology: The Logic of Emotional World Views," *Inquiry* 21 (1978): 194.
33. *Ibid.,* p. 194.

Chapter 5. Religious Belief and Emotional Transformation

1. Most of the philosophical literature on forgiveness focuses on the contrast between forgiveness and pardon and mercy. See, for example, P. Twambley, "Mercy and Forgiveness," *Analysis* 36 (1975): 84–90; H. J. N. Horsbrugh, "Forgiveness," *Canadian Journal of Philosophy* 4 (1974): 269–82; Martin Golding, "Forgiveness and Regret," *Philosophical Forum* 16 (1984): 121–37. My discussion of forgiveness is also heavily indebted to Susan Owen's unpublished manuscript on forgiveness.
2. R. S. Downie has suggested a similar point in "Forgiveness," *Philosophical Quarterly* 15 (1965): 128–34.
3. One does not need to accept the presuppositions about human life identified in the circumstances of justice to endorse a view of moral relations which highlights the claims of individuals to their due. Bishop Butler, for example, seems to have accepted the importance of individual claims to justice without accepting the view of human life articulated in the circumstances of justice.
4. David Hume, *Treatise of Human Nature* (Oxford: Oxford University Press, 1967), p. 494.
5. James Gustafson, *Ethics from a Theocentric Perspective,* p. 96.
6. I owe this formulation of the point to an article by John P. Reeder, Jr. See his "Assenting to Agape," *The Journal of Religion* 60 (1980): 17–31.
7. Again, it is this sort of revision, I think, that lies behind the familiar claim that the good man cannot be harmed.
8. Aurel Kolnai, "Forgiveness," *Proceedings of the Aristotelian Society* 74 (1973–74): 98–99.
9. Although this view may at first appear counterintuitive, it is, I think, a common

theme in literature. A classic expression of this view is found, for example, in Dostoevsky's, *The Brothers Karamazov,* trans. Andrew MacAndrew (New York: Bantam Books, 1970). In Book V, "Pro and Contra," Ivan, despairing about the existence of God, confronts Alyosha with his collection of stories of crimes against children. Such crimes, he feels, cannot be forgiven for Ivan refuses to accept the reunion which would take place with the perpetrators of these crimes were they to be forgiven. Forgiveness, he says, is moral outrage. Ivan is adamant, he cannot forgive the man who viciously set the hounds on the little child because the reconciliation—as he puts it, the "harmony"—that forgiving implies is unthinkable. "No," Ivan says, "I want no part of any harmony; I don't want it, out of love for mankind." Professor Sumner Twiss has pointed out to me that it is possible to read both the section on Ivan's rebellion and the story of the Grand Inquisitor as the presentation of Ivan's case against God based on considerations of human justice. Dostoevsky's point, of course, is that God's love transcends human justice.

10. See Frederick S. Carney, "Accountability in Christian Morality," *The Journal of Religion* 53 (1973): 309–29.

11. Soren Kierkegaard, *Works of Love* (New York: Harper and Row, 1962), p. 209.

12. *Ibid.,* p. 209; my emphasis.

Conclusion

1. See, for example, Robert C. Roberts, *Spirituality and Human Emotion* (Grand Rapids, Mich.: Eerdmans, 1982) and Don Saliers, *The Soul in Paraphrase* (New York: Seabury, 1980).

Bibliography

Religious Studies/Theology

Aquinas, Thomas. *Summa Theologiae*. v. 19–22, la, 2ae, Qq 22–54. New York: McGraw-Hill, 1967.

Berger, Peter. "On the Obsolescence of the Concept of Honor. " In *Revisions: Changing Perspectives in Moral Philosophy*, edited by Stanley Hauerwas and Alasdair MacIntyre, 172–81. Notre Dame, Ind.: University of Notre Dame Press, 1983.

Butler, Joseph. *The Works of Bishop Butler*. London: Macmillan and Co. , 1900 .

Cannon, Katie G. *Black Womanist Ethics*. Atlanta, Ga.: Scholars Press, 1988.

Carney, Frederick. "Accountability in Christian Morality. " *Journal of Religion* 53 (1973): 309–29.

_____. "The Virtue-Obligation Controversy. " *Journal of Religious Ethics* 1 (1973): 5–20.

Dyck, Arthur J. "A Unified Theory of Virtue and Obligation. " *Journal of Religious Ethics* 1 (1973): 37–52.

Edwards, Jonathan. *Works of Jonathan Edwards*. Vol. 2. ed. John E. Smith. New Haven: Yale University Press, 1957.

Evans, Donald. *The Logic of Self-Involvement*. London: SCM Press, 1963.

_____. *Struggle and Fulfillment: The Inner Dynamics of Religion and Morality*. Cleveland, Ohio: Collins, 1979.

Frankena, William K. "The Ethics of Love Conceived as an Ethics of Virtue. " *Journal of Religious Ethics* 1 (1973): 21–36.

Gustafson, James M. *Can Ethics Be Christian?* Chicago: University of Chicago Press, 1975.

_____. *Christ and the Moral Life*. New York: Harper and Row, 1968.

_____. *Ethics from a Theocentric Perspective*. Vols. 1 and 2. Chicago: University of Chicago Press, 1981.

Harak, G. Simon. "The Passions, the Virtues, and Agency: Modern Research and Thomistic Reflection. " *Logos* 8 (1987): 31–44.

Hauerwas, Stanley. *Character and the Christian Life: A Study in Theological Ethics*. San Antonio, Tex.: Trinity University Press, 1975.

_____. *A Community of Character: Toward a Constructive Christian Social Ethics*. Notre Dame, Ind.: University of Notre Dame Press, 1981.

_____. "Ethics and Ascetical Theology. " *Anglican Theological Review* 61 (1979): 87–98.

_____. "Forgiveness and Political Community. " *Worldview* 23/1–2 (1980).

_____. *The Peaceable Kingdom: A Primer in Christian Ethics*. Notre Dame, Ind.: University of Notre Dame Press, 1983.

_____. *Truthfulness and Tragedy: Further Investigations in Christian Ethics*. Notre Dame, Ind.: University of Notre Dame Press, 1977.

_____. *Vision and Virtue: Essays in Christian Ethical Reflection*. Notre Dame, Ind.: Fides Publishers, 1974.

James, William. *The Varieties of Religious Experience: A Study in Human Nature*. New York: Collier, 1961.

Kierkegaard, Soren. *Works of Love*. New York: Harper and Row, 1962.

Lauritzen, Paul. "Emotions and Religious Ethics. " *Journal of Religious Ethics* 16 (1988): 307–24.

_____. "A Feminist Ethic and the New Romanticism—Mothering as a Model of Moral Relations." *Hypatia* 4 (1989): 29–44.

Milhaven, J. Giles. *Good Anger*. Kansas City, Mo.: Sheed and Ward, 1989.

Ogletree, Thomas W. "Character and Narrative: Stanley Hauerwas' Studies of the Christian Life. " *Religious Studies Review* 6 (1980): 25–30.

_____. "Values, Obligations and Virtues: Approaches to Bio-Medical Ethics. " *Journal of Religious Ethics* 4 (1976): 105–30.

Outka, Gene. *Agape: An Ethical Analysis*. New Haven: Yale University Press, 1972.

Owen, Susan. "Repentance and Forgiveness," M. A. Thesis. University of Virginia, 1981.

Proudfoot, Wayne. *Religious Experience*. Berkeley: University of California Press, 1985.

_____. "Religious Experience, Emotion and Belief. " *Harvard Theological Review* 70/3–4 (1977): 343–67.

Reeder, John P. , Jr. "Assenting to Agape. " *The Journal of Religion* 60 (1980): 17–31.

Roberts, Robert C. *Spirituality and Human Emotion*. Grand Rapids, Mich.: Eerdmans, 1982.

Saliers, Don. *The Soul in Paraphrase: Prayer and Religious Affections*. New York: Seabury, 1980.

Schumaker, Millard. *Moral Poise: Toward a Christian Ethic Without Resentment*. Edmonton, Canada: St. Stephen's College, 1977.

Smith, Wilfred Cantwell. *Faith and Belief*. Princeton, N.J.: Princeton University Press, 1979.

Stout, Jeffrey. *The Flight from Authority: Religion, Morality, and the Quest for Autonomy*. Notre Dame, Ind.: University of Notre Dame Press, 1981.

von Hildebrand, Dietrich. "The Role of Affectivity in Morality. " *Proceedings of the Catholic Philosophical Association* 32 (1958): 85–95.

_____. *Transformation in Christ*. New York: Image, 1963.

Philosophical Psychology/ Moral Theory

Aristotle. *The "Art" of Rhetoric*. Trans. by John Henry Freese. London: William Heinemann, 1926.

Baier, Annette. *Postures of the Mind: Essays on Mind and Morals*. Minneapolis: University of Minnesota Press, 1985.

Baillie, Harold W. "Learning the Emotions. " *New Scholasticism* 62 (1988): 221–27.

Ben-Zeev, Aaron. "The Nature of Emotions. " *Philosophical Studies* 52 (1987): 393–409.

Blum, Lawrence. *Friendship. Altruism and Morality.* Boston: Routledge and Kegan Paul, 1980.

Calhoun, Cheshire. "Responsibility and Reproach. " *Ethics* 99 (1989): 389–406.

Callan, Eamonn. "The Moral Status of Pity. " *Canadian Journal of Philosophy* 18 (1988): 1–12.

Callahan, Sidney. "The Role of Emotion in Ethical Decisionmaking. " *Hastings Center Report* 18 (1988): 9–14.

Cartwright, David. "Kant's View of the Moral Significance of Kindhearted Emotions and the Moral Insignificance of Kant's View. " *Journal of Value Inquiry* 21 (1987): 291–304.

Culler, Jonathan. *On Deconstruction: Theory and Criticism After Structuralism.* Ithaca: Cornell University Press, 1982.

DeSousa, Ronald. *The Rationality of Emotion.* Cambridge: MIT Press, 1987.

Downie, Robert Silcock. "Forgiveness. " *Philosophical Quarterly* 15 (1965): 128–34.

Feinberg, Joel. *Doing and Deserving*: *Essays in the Theory of Responsibility.* Princeton, N.J.: Princeton University Press, 1970.

_____. *Rights, Justice, and the Bounds of Liberty*: *Essays in Social Philosophy.* Princeton, N.J.: Princeton University Press, 1980.

Fortenbaugh, W. W. *Aristotle on Emotion*: *A Contribution to Philosophical Psychology, Rhetoric, Poetics, Politics, and Ethics.* London: Duckworth, 1975.

Frankena, William. "Prichard and the Ethics of Virtue, Notes on a Footnote. " *Monist* 54 (1970): 1–17.

Gingell, John. "Forgiveness and Power. " *Analysis* 34 (1974).

Golding, Martin. "Forgiveness and Regret. " *Philosophical Forum* 16 (1984): 121–37.

Gordon, Robert. "The Aboutness of Emotions. " *American Philosophical Quarterly* 11 (1974): 27–36.

_____. "Emotions and Knowledge. " *Journal of Philosophy* 66 (1969): 408–13.

_____. "Judgmental Emotions. " *Analysis* 34 (1973): 40–49.

Greenspan, Patricia. *Emotions and Reasons*: *An Inquiry into Emotional Justification.* New York: Routledge, 1988.

Greenspan, Patricia. "Emotions, Reasons and Self-Involvement. " *Philosophical Studies* 38 (1980): 161–68.

Hampshire, Stuart. *Freedom of Mind and Other Essays.* Princeton, N.J.: Princeton University Press, 1971.

_____. "Morality and Pessimism. " In *Public and Private Morality*, ed. Stuart Hampshire, Cambridge: Cambridge University Press, 1978.

_____. *Thought and Action.* London: Chatto Windus, 1982.

Hepburn, R. W. "The Arts and the Education of Feelings and Emotion." In *Education and the Development of Reason*, ed. R. F. Dearden, P. H. Hirst, and R. S. Peters, 1–22. London: Routledge and Kegan Paul, 1972.

Horsbrugh, H. J. N. "Forgiveness. " *Canadian Journal of Philosophy* 4 (1974): 269–82.

Hume, David. *A Treatise of Human Nature.* Oxford: Oxford University Press, 1967.

Kant, Immanuel. *Anthropology from a Pragmatic Point of View.* trans. by Mary Gregor. The Hague: Martinus Nijhoff, 1974.

_____. *The Critique of Judgment.* trans. by James Meredith. Oxford: Clarendon Press, 1952.

_____. *Foundations of the Metaphysics of Morals and What Is Enlightenment.* trans. by Lewis White Beck. Indianapolis, Ind.: Bobbs-Merrill, 1959.

Bibliography 123

_____. *Metaphysical Principles of Virtue.* trans. by James Ellington (1964. reprint. Indianapolis: Hackett, 1983).

Kolnai, Aurel. "Forgiveness." *Proceedings of the Aristotelian Society* 74 (1973–74): 91–106.

Leighton, Stephen R. "Unfelt Feelings in Pain and Emotion. "*The Southern Journal of Philosophy* 24 (1986): 69–79.

_____. "The New View of Emotions. " *American Philosophical Quarterly* 22 (1985): 133–41.

Lewis, Meirlys. "On Forgiveness." *Philosophical Quarterly* 30 (1980): 236–245.

Lyons, William. *Emotion.* Cambridge: Cambridge University Press, 1980.

MacIntyre, Alasdair. *After Virtue: A Study in Moral Theory.* Notre Dame, Ind.: University of Notre Dame Press, 1981.

Mackie, John. "Morality and the Retributive Emotions." *Acta Philosophica Fennica* 34 (1982): 144–57.

Midgley, Mary. *Beast and Man: The Roots of Human Nature.* Ithaca: Cornell University Press, 1978.

_____. *Heart and Mind: The Varieties of Moral Experience.* New York: St. Martin's Press, 1981.

Mischel, Theodore, ed. *Cognitive Development and Epistemology.* New York: Academic Press, 1981.

_____, ed. *Human Action: Conceptual and Empirical Issues.* New York: Academic Press, 1969.

_____. "Kant and the Possibility of a Science of Psychology. " *Monist* 51 (1967): 599–622.

_____. "Psychological Explanations and Their Vicissitudes." In Nebraska *Symposium on Motivation,* vol. 23, edited by W. J. Arnold, 133–204. Lincoln: University of Nebraska Press, 1976.

_____ , ed. *The Self—Psychological and Philosophical Issues.* Totowa, N.J.: Rowman & Littlefield, 1977.

Mitchell, Basil, ed. *Philosophy of Religion.* London: Oxford University Press, 1971.

Montaigne, Michel. *The Complete Essays.* Trans. by Donald Frame. Stanford, Calif.: Stanford University Press, 1965.

Murphy, Jeffrey. "Forgiveness and Resentment. " *Midwest Studies in Philosophy,* 7 (1982): 503–16.

Neu, Jerome. *Emotion. Thought and Therapy: A Study of Hume and Spinoza and the Relationship of Philosophical Theories of the Emotions to Psychological Theories of Therapy.* Berkeley: University of California Press, 1977.

Nussbaum, Martha C. *The Fragility of Goodness.* Cambridge: Cambridge University Press, 1986.

O'Shaughnessy, R. J. "Forgiveness." *Philosophy* 42 (1967): 336–52.

Perkins, Moreland. "Emotion and Feeling." *Philosophical Review* 75 (1966): 139–60.

Peters, Richard Stanley. "Emotions, Passivity and the Place of Freud's Theory in Psychology." In *Scientific Psychology: Principles and Approaches,* edited by Benjamin Wolman and Ernest Nagel, 365–83. New York: Basic Books, 1965.

_____. "Emotions and the Category of Passivity." *Proceedings of the Aristotelian Society* 62 (1961–62): 117–42.

_____. *Reason and Compassion.* London: Routledge & Kegan Paul, 1973.

Phillips, Dewi. *Through a Darkening Glass.* Notre Dame, Ind.: University of Notre Dame Press, 1982.

Pitcher, George. "Emotion." *Mind* 74 (1965): 326–46.

Prichard, Harold Arthur. *Moral Obligation: Essays and Lectures.* London: Oxford University Press, 1949.

Pritchard, Michael S. "Human Dignity and Justice." *Ethics* 82 (1972): 299–313.

Rawls, John. *A Theory of Justice.* Cambridge: Harvard University Press, 1971.

Roberts, Robert C. "What an Emotion Is: A Sketch." *Philosophical Review* 97 (1988) 183–209.

Rorty, Amelie, ed. *Explaining Emotions.* Berkeley: University of California Press, 1980.

_____. "From Passions to Emotions and Sentiments." *Philosophy* 57 (1982):159–72.

Sachs, David. "On Freud's Doctrine of Emotions." In *Freud: A Collection of Critical Essays,* edited by Richard Wollhem, 132–46. New York: Doubleday Anchor, 1974.

Sandel, Michael. *Liberalism and the Limits of Justice.* Cambridge: Cambridge University Press, 1982.

Scheler, Max. *Ressentiment.* New York: Free Press of Glencoe, 1961.

Scheman, Naomi. "Anger and the Politics of Naming." In *Women and Language in Literature and Society,* edited by Ruth Borker, Sally McConnell-Ginet, and Nelly Furman, 174–87. New York: Praeger, 1980.

_____. "On Sympathy." *Monist* 62 (1979): 320–30.

Schoeman, Ferdinand, ed. *Responsibility, Character, and the Emotions: New Essays in Moral Psychology.* Cambridge: Cambridge University Press, 1987.

Schrader, George. "The Structure of Emotion." In *Invitation to Phenomenology: Studies in the Philosophy of Experience,* edited by James. Edie, 252–65. Chicago: Quadrangle, 1965.

Searle, John. *Speech Acts: An Essay in the Philosophy of Language.* Cambridge: Cambridge University Press, 1969.

Seidler, Michael. "Kant and the Stoics on the Emotional Life." *Philosophy Research Archives* 7 (1981): 1093–1108.

Solomon, Robert C. "Emotions and Anthropology: The Logic of Emotional World Views." *Inquiry* 21 (1978): 181–99.

_____. "On Emotions as Judgments." *American Philosophical Quarterly* 25 (1988): 183–91.

_____. "L'Etranger and the Truth." *Philosophy and Literature* 2 (1978): 141–59.

_____. "The Logic of Emotion." *Nous* 11 (1977): 41–49.

_____. *A Passion for Justice: Emotions and the Origins of the Social Contract.* Reading, Mass.: Addison-Wesley, 1990.

_____. *The Passions: The Myth and Nature of Human Emotions.* New York: Anchor Press, 1976.

_____. "Paul Ricoeur on Passion and Emotion." In *Studies in the Philosophy of Paul Ricoeur,* edited by Charles Reagan, 2–20. Athens, Ohio: Ohio University Press, 1979.

Strawson, Peter. *Freedom and Resentment and Other Essays.* London: Methuen, 1974.

Taylor, Charles. *The Explanation of Behavior.* New York: Humanities Press, 1964.

_____. *Human Agency and Language.* Vol 1. of the *Philosophical Papers of Charles Taylor.* Cambridge: Cambridge University Press, 1985.

_____. *Philosophy and the Human Sciences.* Vol. 2 of the *Philosophical Papers of Charles Taylor.* Cambridge: Cambridge University Press, 1985.

_____. *Sources of the Self—The Making of the Modern Identity.* Cambridge: Harvard University Press, 1989.

Thalberg, Irving. "Constituents and Causes of Emotion and Action." *Philosophical Quarterly* 23 (1973): 1–14.

_____. "Emotion and Thought." *American Philosophical Quarterly* 1 (1964): 45–55.

Twambley, P. "Mercy and Forgiveness." *Analysis* 36 (1975) 84–90.

Unger, Roberto Mangabeira. *Passion: An Essay on Personality*. New York: The Free Press, 1984.

Warnock, Mary. "The Justification of Emotions." *Proceedings of the Aristotelian Society*, Supp. 31 (1957): 43–74.

Williams, Bernard. *Moral Luck: Philosophical Papers. 1973–1980*. Cambridge: Cambridge University Press, 1981.

_____. *Problems of the Self: Philosophical Papers. 1956–1972*. Cambridge: Cambridge University Press, 1973.

Wilson, John. *Emotion and Object*. Cambridge: Cambridge University Press, 1972.

Winch, Peter. *The Idea of a Social Science and Its Relation to Philosophy*. London: Routledge & Kegan Paul, 1958.

Wittgenstein, Ludwig. *Philosophical Investigations*. trans. by G. E. M. Anscombe. New York: Macmillan, 1953.

_____. *Remarks on the Philosophy of Psychology*. 2 volumes. Chicago: University of Chicago Press, 1980.

Psychology

Averill, James. *Anger and Aggression: An Essay on Emotion*. New York: Springer-Verlag, 1982.

_____. "Emotions and Anxiety: Sociological, Biological and Psychological Determinants." In *Emotions and Anxiety: New Concepts. Methods. and Applications*, edited by Marvin Zuckerman and Charles Spielberger, 87–103. Hillsdale, N.J.: Lawrence Erlbaum, 1976.

Hearst, Eliot, ed. *The First Century of Experimental Psychology*. Hillsdale, N. J. : Lawrence Erlbaum, 1979.

James, William. *The Principles of Psychology*. New York: Holt and Co., 1905 .

James, William, and Carl Georg Lange. *The Emotions*. Baltimore: Williams and Wilkins, 1922.

Lazarus, Richard S. "On the Primacy of Cognition." *American Psychologist* 39 (1984): 124–29.

_____. "Thoughts on the Relations Between Emotion and Cognition." *American Psychologist* 37 (1982): 1019–24.

Lazarus, R., and J. Averill. "Emotion and Cognition." In *Anxiety: Current Trends in Theory and Research*, edited by Charles Spielberger, vol. 2, 242–90. New York: Academic Press, 1972.

Lazarus, Richard S., James C. Coyne, and Susan Folkman. "Cognition, Emotion and Motivation: The Doctoring of Humpty-Dumpty." In *Approaches to Emotion*, edited by Klaus Scherer and Paul Ekman, 221–37. Hillsdale, N.J.: Lawrence Erlbaum, 1984.

Mandler, George. "Emotion." In *The First Century of Experimental Psychology*, edited by Eliot Hearst, 275–321. Hillsdale, N.J.: Lawrence Erlbaum, 1979.

_____. "A Reassessment of the 'Primacy of Affect.'" *Cognitive Therapy and Research* 8 (1984): 579–84.

Rachman, S. "The Primacy of Affect." *Behaviour Research and Therapy* 19 (1981): 279–90.

Schachter, S., and J. E. Singer. "Cognitive, Social and Physiological Determinants of Emotional State." *Psychological Review* 69 (1962): 379–99.

Scherer, Klaus. "Emotions Can Be Rational." *Social Science Information* 24 (1985) 331–35.

Scherer, Klaus, and Paul Ekman, ed. *Approaches to Emotion*. Hillsdale, N.J.: Lawrence Erlbaum, 1984.

Shaver, Phillip, ed. *Review of Personality and Social Psychology: Emotions, Relationships, and Health*. Beverly Hills, Calif.: Sage, 1984.

_____. "On the Primacy of Affect." *American Psychologist* 39 (1984): 117–23.

Zajonc, R. B. "Feeling and Thinking: Preferences Need No Inferences." *American Psychologist* 35 (1980) 151–75.

Social Sciences

Briggs, Jean. *Never in Anger: Portrait of an Eskimo Family*. Cambridge: Harvard University Press, 1970.

Geertz, Clifford. *The Interpretation of Cultures*. New York: Basic Books, 1973.

Gergen, Kenneth ed. *The Social Construction of the Person*. New York: Springer-Verlag, 1985.

Greenwood, John D. "Emotion and Error." *Philosophy of the Social Sciences* 17 (1987): 487–99.

Harris, Grace Gredys. *Casting out Anger: Religion among the Taita of Kenya*. Cambridge: Cambridge University Press, 1978.

Heelas, Paul, and Andrew Lock. *Indigenous Psychologies: The Anthropology of the Self*. London: Academic Press, 1981.

Hochschild, Arlie Russell. *The Managed Heart: Commercialization of Human Feeling*. Berkeley: University of California Press, 1983.

Leites, Edmund. *The Puritan Conscience and Modern Sexuality*. New Haven: Yale University Press, 1986.

Levy, Robert I. and Michelle Z. Rosaldo, ed. *Ethos* 11 (1983): 27–213. Issue of the journal *Ethos* devoted to "Self and Emotion."

Lutz, Catherine A. *Unnatural Emotions—Everyday Sentiments on a Micronesian Atoll and Their Challenge to Western Theory*. Chicago: University of Chicago Press, 1988.

Plattner, Stuart. *Text, Play, and Story: The Construction and Reconstruction of Self and Society*. Washington: American Ethnological Society, 1984.

_____. "Toward an Anthropology of Self and Feeling." In *Culture Theory: Essays on Mind. Self. and Emotion*, edited by Richard A. Shweder and Robert A. LeVine, 137–57. Cambridge: Cambridge University Press, 1984.

Rosaldo, Michelle Zimbalist. *Knowledge and Passion: Ilongot Notions of Self and Social Life*. Cambridge: Cambridge University Press, 1980.

Stearns, Carol Z., and Peter N. Stearns. *Anger: The Struggle for Emotional Control in America's History*. Chicago: University of Chicago Press, 1986.

Stearns, Peter N., and Carol Z. Stearns. "Emotionology: Clarifying the History of Emotions and Emotional Standards." *American Historical Review* 90 (1985): 813–36.

Zeldin, Theodore. "Personal History and the History of the Emotions." *Journal of Social History* 15 (1982): 339–47.

Index

Anger: circumstances of justice and, 94–96, 99–100, 104; everyday example of, 69–71; *Grapes of Wrath* and, 78–86; hydraulic metaphors and, 58, 68, 69, 75; in non-Western cultures, 75–78, 88–89; self-understanding and, 72, 73, 89, 94, 96, 98, 101; social norms of, 72–75
Averill, James, 62, 64, 65, 70

Briggs, Jean, 88, 89
Butler, Bishop, 87– 88, 97–98

Carney, Frederick, 104

Death of Ivan Ilych, 43, 47
Duty, ethic of, 14, 16, 17, 22

Emotion: constructivist theory of, 19, 50, 57–58, 61; definition of, 65; dichotomy with reason and, 7, 14–15, 19, 27, 53, 108; intentional character of, 55, 65; noncognitivist view of, 50–55, 57; rules and, 62–64, 73–74; self-understanding and, 42–45; as text, 59–62, 66

Forgiveness: circumstances of justice and, 95–96, 99; definition of, 93–94; as duty, 91, 102–4
Frankena, William, 21
Freud, Sigmund, 75

Geertz, Clifford, 19, 57–58, 65–66, 109
Grapes of Wrath, 78–79, 86

Gustafson, James, 14–15, 97

Hampshire, Stuart, 56
Harris, Grace Gredys, 75–76
Hauerwas, Stanley: self-understanding and, 16, 25–26, 31–32; standard account of rationality and, 23–27; virtue theory and, 16, 22–23, 30
Hume, David, 94

James, William, 51–56
Justice: circumstances of, 94–96, 99, 104; retributive framework of, 94–100

Kant, Immanuel, 23, 28–30, 97
Kierkegaard, Soren, 105–6
Kolnai, Aurel, 102–3

MacIntyre, Alasdair, 16, 18, 31, 32
Midgley, Mary, 27

Narrative: self-understanding and, 24–25, 31–33, 40, 48

Passion: hermeneutics of, 60–61, 65–66. *See also* Emotion
Prichard, H. A., 13–14, 17

Reason: dichotomy with emotion and, 7, 14–15, 19, 27, 53, 108
Resentment: Butler's account of, 87–88
Rosaldo, Michelle, 58–59, 75

Sandel, Michael, 39

127